Create Your Own Operating Systems for the Internet of Things

By Lucus Darnell

Disclaimer

I have spent a lot of extremely late nights writing this book. So, if you find any errors within this book, please feel free to send me an email at the address below so that I can correct those errors and help you resolve any problems you might have.

With that said, the information in this book is for educational purposes only. Neither the author nor the publisher are responsible or liable for any direct, indirect, consequential, or incidental loss, damage, injury, or other issues that may result or arise from the use, misuse, or abuse of the information provided in this book.

ISBN-13: 978-1981624058

Table of Contents

Create Your Own Operating System

Lucus Darnell

Introduction

Take a look around you right now and count how many electronic devices you can see from your current point of view. If you are like most people, you probably have numerous devices just within your current eye sight. In order for many of those devices to work, they have some sort of operating system (OS) that allows them to boot up and provide whatever experiences it is they have to offer. In fact, if you are reading the digital version of this book, the very device you are now holding has an operating system of its own.

However, not all electronic devices have an operating system. For example, most microwave ovens do not have an OS since they only have a small set of tasks to perform with very little input (in the form of a keypad) to process and no chance of the hardware changing. Operating systems would typically be overkill for devices like this as they would increase development and manufacturing costs and add complexity where none is required.

With that said, technologies are getting smaller, cheaper, and faster which is providing manufacturers the ability to leverage full-blown operating systems for handling more processing and adding additional functionality in their devices. Take the microwave oven from before as an example. Even devices such as these are beginning to be connected to the *Internet of Things*[1] (IoT) so that manufacturers can track the usage (and issues) with their devices even after they have been purchased and installed in our homes. Plus, IoT-enabled devices such as the "connected microwave" allows the end user - the consumer in this case - to monitor and manage their own devices remotely and autonomously. Devices with this capability require an operating system to handle the connectivity to the Internet along with whatever base functionality the devices already provide.

[1] If you would like to learn more about the *Internet of Things* and explore various real-world use cases, please check out my book on Amazon aptly titled, "*The Internet of Things: A Look at Real-World Use Cases and Concerns*" which you can find at http://www.amazon.com/gp/product/B017M7S0A0

Recently I started working on a new project for the *Internet of Things* that involves the need for an entirely new operating system. Unfortunately, my C programming skills were a bit rusty and it had been more than fifteen years since I had written anything in Assembly. So, in order for me to brush up on my C and Assembly skills I needed to build a new operating system, I did like any good programmer would do and I turned to the Internet. The first place I began my search was amazon.com. I was hoping that I would find a decent book that could help me along with my project. However, to my surprise, I could only find one book that is dedicated to developing an operating system from scratch and it has some pretty nasty reviews. That was when I decided to write my own book that will hopefully help the next generation of programmers get back to the roots of developing software by explaining the fundamentals of how computers actually work all while building toward the end goal of having your own operating system.

Despite what the forum trolls will tell you, writing your own operating system is actually quite easy. The tough part comes when it is time to expand your OS. Since you are building a completely new operating system, you will not have the luxury of utilizing readily available libraries that existing operating systems provide out-of-the-box. That means that for every little piece of extra functionality to even the most basic of system calls, you will have to write every last bit from scratch. If you continue working on your OS, over time you will develop a good size library that rivals some of the operating systems that exist today.

For the purposes of this book, I will walk you through the step-by-step process of building and running your very own operating system for the x86 processor. Why the x86 processor? Well, this decision is made based on the fact that there are already plenty of x86 based computers available in which you can get your feet wet. Plus, there are lots of websites out there to help you should you get stuck with anything further down the road. Even though the operating system you will learn to develop in this book is intended for the x86 processor, you can use these same techniques for building an OS for other types of processors as well, which I will explain in a later chapter.

One assumption I will make throughout this book is that you already have a fair amount of understanding for how computers work. For readers that do, a few of the chapters in this book will basically be refreshers. For readers that are completely new to programming and/or how computers work, you will most likely find some of the things mentioned herein a little difficult to follow. However, I will still do my best to (re)introduce certain concepts to you to help illustrate what we are trying to achieve in this book. Regardless of your knowledge and skill level, I hope that you will find the following text educational, informative, and useful. With that said, let's dive right in.

Create Your Own Operating System

0x01 OS Basics

Before we jump into building the next Windows, Linux, Android, OS X, iOS, or other fancy operating system, we need to begin by examining what an operating system is and how it works in the first place. To begin with, the operating system (OS) is the primary piece of software that sits between the physical hardware and the applications used by the end user (such as Word and Excel).

The most popular operating systems are those mentioned above where Windows, Linux, and OS X are the most common operating systems for desktop & laptop computers. Variations of Linux (along with Unix) are also responsible for powering the majority of high-end servers such as those that power the Internet while Android and iOS are [currently] the two most popular operating systems for powering mobile devices such as smartphones and tablets.

The primary responsibility of the operating system is to provide a common way for applications to work with hardware regardless of who manufactures that hardware and what it includes. For example, a laptop computer contains different hardware than that found in a desktop computer. Both types of computers can also have different amounts of memory, processor speeds, and peripherals. Instead of requiring software developers to build their applications to support all of these various pieces of hardware, the operating system abstracts that away by providing an interface that the applications can interact with in a common way, regardless of what the underlying hardware looks like.

Since the primary responsibility of the operating system is to provide a common interface for applications to interact with the physical hardware (and with each other), it is also the OS's job to make sure that all applications are treated equally so that they can each utilize the hardware when necessary.

In order for any software (including the operating system) to run, it has to first be loaded into memory where the Central Processing Unit (CPU) can access and execute it. At first, the software starts out residing on some sort of storage device - be it a hard disk drive (HDD), solid state drive (SSD), CD or DVD, SD card, thumb drive, or other type of flash memory device or ROM - but is moved into memory when the system is ready to operate with the relevant piece of software.

In general, the operating system is responsible for several tasks. The first task that the operating system is responsible for is managing the usage of the processor. It works by dividing the processor's work into manageable chunks. Next, it prioritizes these chunks before sending them to the CPU for processing and execution.

The second task the OS is responsible for is memory management. Depending on the purpose and needs of the operating system, memory management can be handled in different ways. The first is what is known as "single contiguous allocation". This is where just enough memory for running the operating system is reserved for the OS while the rest is made available to a single application (such as MS-DOS and embedded systems).

The second type of memory management is known as "partitioned allocation". This is where the memory is divided into multiple partitions and each partition is allocated to a specific job or task and is unallocated (freed) when the job is complete and the memory can be re-allocated to other tasks.

The third type of memory management is known as "paged management". This is where the system divides all of its memory into equal fixed-sized units called "page frames". As applications are loaded, their virtual address spaces are then divided into pages of the same size.

The fourth type of memory management is known as "segmented management". This is where the system takes a "chunk" of an application (such as a function) and loads it into a memory segment by itself. This memory segment is allocated based on the size of the "chunk" being loaded and prevents other applications from accessing the same memory space.

After the operating system has setup the memory to accept code to be executed, it then moves its attention to managing the rest of the hardware. For example, the OS is responsible for interpreting input from peripherals such as the mouse and keyboard so that the applications that depend on these devices can interact with them in a uniform fashion. It is also responsible for sending output to the monitor at the correct resolution as well as configuring the network interface if available.

Next, the operating system takes care of managing devices for storing data. Persisting data to long term storage is absolutely necessary for user-based operating systems such as Windows, Linux, and OS X, but isn't necessarily required for other operating systems such as those that run on embedded devices.

Aside from managing the physical hardware and providing an interface for applications to work with said hardware, the operating system is also responsible for providing a user interface (UI) which is what allows the user to interact with the system. The user interface that the operating system provides is also [typically] what defines how the applications running on the OS look as well.

To better understand where the operating system sits in relation to the rest of the system and to better understand its responsibilities, the following image should help.

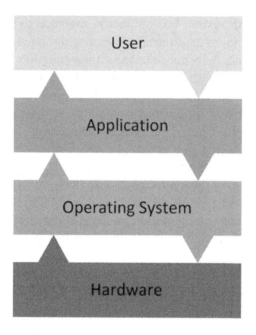

As you can see (looking at the image from the bottom up), all computer systems begin with the bare metal hardware. The operating system sits on top of the hardware and acts as a manager of the hardware. As mentioned before, it is also responsible for interfacing applications (the software we use) with said hardware. At the top of it all is the user. Whenever a task needs to be performed by the system, the user feeds input into the system via hardware peripherals such as a mouse and keyboard. This input is then read in by the operating system and passed up to the application which provides the code for performing whatever task is expected by the user. After the application has completed its tasks, it passes its output back to the operating system where it is passed back to the hardware in the form of feedback to the user. This feedback can come in various forms such as text and images on a monitor, sounds from the speakers, or other output via tactile devices.

0x02 Intro to Machine Code

At its most basic level, a computer works by pushing a string of numbers into memory where the CPU can process those numbers. Depending on what those numbers are and what sequence they are ordered in, the computer will read those numbers and perform different tasks. When these numbers, are passed into memory, they take on the form of higher and lower voltage. When these numbers are passed into the CPU, they tell tiny transistors to change their state to be either on or off (again, higher or lower voltage). This shifting in state is what controls something called a "logic gate", which can be either open or closed.

If you noticed, the examples mentioned in the previous paragraph can only take two states: high or low; on or off; open or closed. In order for a computer to understand these states, they are represented as ones and zeros which we call "binary" or "machine code": 10110110, for example. When strings of these zeros and ones are read by the computer, they can cause it to do great things.

Each zero and one found in a binary string represents what is called a "bit". When you group eight bits together, you get what is known as a "byte". One thousand bytes is equal to one kilobyte. One thousand kilobytes is equal to one megabyte. One thousand megabytes is equal to one gigabyte. And so on. In the world of computers that we will be designing our operating system for, a bit can only be a one or a zero as explained above. However, in the world of quantum computing, a "quantum bit" (also known as a "qubit" for short) can be a one or a zero or both at the same time. But, I will leave that for another book.

Originally, bits were grouped together in threes with each bit being on or off and representing eight numbers from 0 to 7: 000 = 0; 001 = 1; 010 = 2; 011 = 3; 100 = 4; 101 = 5; 110 = 6; 111 = 7. This is what is known as "octal" (meaning 8). As computers became more powerful, engineers found that by grouping bits together four at a time instead, they could double the number of possibilities which gives us the number 16 and where we get hexadecimal: "hex" meaning 6 and "decimal" meaning 10. We will learn about decimal and hexadecimal shortly.

To the untrained eye, a string of zeros and ones looks like ... well ... a string of zeros and ones. But, these zeros and ones can be crunched at incredible speeds by a computer where endless calculations can be performed. However, since humans can't crunch the zeros and ones as fast as a computer can, we choose to use other ways to represent these numbers. Plus, by using other representations for machine code and by using the same simple mathematics that we learned as children, we too can perform the same calculations as the computer, just not as fast.

To keep things simple for us humans, we like to use the base-10 numerical system when counting. This numerical system is known as the "decimal" numeral system because "dec" in "decimal" actually means "10". The "base" part, also known as "radix", represents the number of different digits or combinations of digits and letters a system uses to represent letters. For example, in the decimal counting system, everything begins with a derivative of 10, with 0 being the lowest possible value, and counting upward 10 places (i.e. 0, 1, 2, 3, 4, 5, 6, 7, 8, 9). Once we have counted 10 places, the numerical system starts over again and increments by 10 each time it starts over and so on (i.e. **10**, 11, 12, 13, 14, 15, 16, 17, 18, 19, **20** .... 96, 97, 98, 99, **100**, 101 ....).

The base-10 numerical system provides us with the simple numbers that we use in everyday life. At the same time, every number we can possibly imagine also has a binary representation. For example, the current year, 2016, can be represented in binary as 00110010001100000011000100110110. However, the use of binary digits (zeros and ones) is also an abstraction. The number "2016" could just as well be an instruction that tells the computer what do, such as load a value from memory into a CPU register. The zeros and ones are simply a way for us to distinguish between two different values which is what we call "boolean logic". It is also what is known as a base-2 system. But, as mentioned before, using a base-10 (decimal) system makes things easier for us humans. Take a look at the following sequence of numbers for example.

---

0 17791 17996 258 1 0 0 0 0 2 62 1 0 176 64 0 0 64 0 0 0 240 0 0 0 0 0 64 56 2 64 4 3 1 0 5 0 0 0 0 0 0 64 0 0 0 64 0 0 205 0 0 0 205 0 0 0 0 32 0 0 1 0 6 0 208 0 0 0 208 96 0 0 208 96 0 0 6 0 0 0 6 0 0 0 0 32 0 0 1722 0 47360 208 96 443 0 47104

4 0 32973 440 0 52480 128 0 30028 30051 2675 11776 26739 29811 29810 25185 11776 25972 29816 11776 24932 24948 0 0 0 0 0 0 0 0 0 0 11 0 1 0 6 0 0 0 176 64 0 0 176 0 0 0 29 0 0 0 0 0 0 16 0 0 0 0 0 0 0 17 0 1 0 3 0 0 0 208 96 0 0 208 0 0 0 6 0 0 0 0 0 0 4 0 0 0 0 0 0 1 0 3 0 0 0 0 0 0 0 0 214 0 0 0 23 0 0 0 0 0 0 1 0 0 0 0 0 0

To you and me, these numbers don't mean a thing. But, to a machine that can speak this language, the numbers are a set of instructions. In this particular case, the numbers above tell the computer to print my name, "Lucus", to a console window. When these numbers are converted from decimal to machine code, that is when they become binary digits in the form of 1's and 0's as mentioned above.

Although humans like to use the base-10 (decimal) system, computers prefer to use a base-16 system instead called "hexadecimal" or "hex" for short (mentioned earlier). Unfortunately, counting sixteen digits and starting over with an additional increment of sixteen like we do with the base-10 system proved to be a hassle when only working with numerical digits. So, the letters A, B, C, D, E, and F were added to the decimal counting system to account for the remaining six digits. Therefore, after counting from 0 to 9, you can substitute the letter A for the number 10, B for the number 11, all the way up to the letter F for 15, giving us a grand total of 16 digits (remember, we start counting with zero).

As per Wikipedia, four bits is known as a "nibble" and a nibble is one hexadecimal digit (i.e. 0-9 or A-F). Two nibbles, or eight bits, make up a byte (i.e. 00 - FF). When you total up all possibilities of 00 - FF combinations, 00 - FF in hexadecimal is equal to 0 - 255 in decimal. Again, this demonstrates how using our base-10 counting system is easier for us humans.

To give you an idea of what programs look like in hexadecimal format, let's take the same number sequence from above and convert all of the decimal values to hexadecimal. When you do the conversion, you will end up with the following.

457f 464c 0102 0001 0000 0000 0000 0000 0002 003e 0001 0000 00b0 0040 0000 0000 0040 0000 0000 0000 00f0 0000 0000 0000 0000 0000 0040 0038 0002 0040 0004 0003 0001 0000 0005 0000 0000 0000 0000 0000 0000 0040 0000 0000 0000 0040 0000 0000 00cd 0000 0000 0000 00cd 0000 0000 0000 0020 0000 0000 0001 0000 0006 0000 00d0 0000 0000 0000 00d0 0060 0000 0000 00d0 0060 0000 0000 0000 0006 0000 0000 0000 0006 0000 0000 0000 0000 0020 0000 0000 06ba 0000 b900 00d0 0060 01bb 0000 b800 0004 0000 80cd 01b8 0000 cd00 0080 0000 754c 7563 0a73 2e00 6873 7473 7472 6261 2e00 6574 7478 2e00 6164 6174 0000 0000 0000 0000 0000 0000 0000 0000 0000 0000 000b 0000 0001 0000 0006 0000 0000 0000 00b0 0040 0000 0000 00b0 0000 0000 0000 001d 0000 0000

0000 0000 0000 0000 0000 0010 0000 0000 0000 0000 0000 0000 0000 0011 0000 0001 0000 0003 0000 0000 0000
00d0 0060 0000 0000 00d0 0000 0000 0000 0006 0000 0000 0000 0000 0000 0000 0004 0000 0000 0000 0000
0000 0000 0000 0001 0000 0003 0000 0000 0000 0000 0000 0000 0000 0000 00d6 0000 0000 0000 0017 0000
0000 0000 0000 0000 0000 0000 0001 0000 0000 0000 0000 0000 0000 0000

Even though this mess isn't any easier to read than the decimal version above, it should at least give you an idea of how hexadecimal works. If you were to take those same hexadecimal values and convert them to binary so that the computer can understand them, you would end up with the following.

```
1000101011111110 1000110010011000 0000001000000100 0000000000000010 0000000000000000
0000000000000000 0000000000000000 0000000000000000 0000000000000100 0000000001111100
0000000000000010 0000000000000000 0000000101100000 0000000010000000 0000000000000000
0000000000000000 0000000001000000 0000000000000000 0000000000000000 0000000000000000
0000000111100000 0000000000000000 0000000000000000 0000000000000000 0000000000000000
0000000000000000 0000000001000000 0000000001110000 0000000000000100 0000000010000000
0000000000001000 0000000000000110 0000000000000010 0000000000000000 0000000000001010
0000000000000000 0000000000000000 0000000000000000 0000000000000000 0000000000000000
0000000000000000 0000000001000000 0000000000000000 0000000000000000 0000000000000000
0000000010000000 0000000000000000 0000000000000000 0000000110011010 0000000000000000
0000000000000000 0000000000000000 0000000110011010 0000000000000000 0000000000000000
0000000000000000 0000000000000000 0000000001000000 0000000000000000 0000000000000000
0000000000000010 0000000000000000 0000000000001100 0000000000000000 0000000110100000
0000000000000000 0000000000000000 0000000000000000 0000000110100000 0000000011000000
0000000000000000 0000000000000000 0000000110100000 0000000011000000 0000000000000000
0000000000000000 0000000000001100 0000000000000000 0000000000000000 0000000000000000
0000000000001100 0000000000000000 0000000000000000 0000000000000000 0000000000000000
0000000001000000 0000000000000000 0000000000000000 0000011010110100 0000000000000001
0111001000000000 0000000110100000 0000000011000000 0000001101110110 0000000000000001
0111000000000000 0000000000001000 0000000000000001 0000000110011010 0000001101110000
0000000000000001 1001101000000000 0000000100000000 0000000000000000 1110101010011000
1110101011000110 0001010011100110 0101110000000000 1101000011100110 1110100011100110
1110100011100100 1100010011000010 0101110000000000 1100101011101000 1110100011110000
0101110000000000 1100001011001000 1100001011101000 0000000000000000 0000000000000000
0000000000000000 0000000000000000 0000000000000000 0000000000000000 0000000000000000
0000000000000000 0000000000000000 0000000000000000 0000000000010110 0000000000000000
0000000000000010 0000000000000000 0000000000001100 0000000000000000 0000000000000000
0000000000000000 0000000101100000 0000000010000000 0000000000000000 0000000000000000
0000000101100000 0000000000000000 0000000000000000 0000000000000000 0000000000111010
0000000000000000 0000000000000000 0000000000000000 0000000000000000 0000000000000000
0000000000000000 0000000000000000 0000000000100000 0000000000000000 0000000000000000
0000000000100010 0000000000000000 0000000000000010 0000000000000000 0000000000000110
0000000000000000 0000000000000000 0000000000000000 0000000110100000 0000000011000000
0000000000000000 0000000000000000 0000000110100000 0000000000000000 0000000000000000
0000000000000000 0000000000001100 0000000000000000 0000000000000000 0000000000000000
0000000000000000 0000000000000000 0000000000000000 0000000000000000 0000000000001000
0000000000000000 0000000000000000 0000000000000000 0000000000000000 0000000000000000
0000000000000000 0000000000000000 0000000000000010 0000000000000000 0000000000000110
0000000000000000 0000000000000000 0000000000000000 0000000000000000 0000000000000000
0000000000000000 0000000000000000 0000000000000000 0000000000000000 0000000110101100
0000000000000000 0000000000000000 0000000000000000 0000000000101110 0000000000000000
0000000000000000 0000000000000000 0000000000000000 0000000000000000 0000000000000000
```

```
0000000000000000 0000000000000010 0000000000000000 0000000000000000 0000000000000000
0000000000000000 0000000000000000 0000000000000000 0000000000000000
```

⌐ ⌐ ⌐ ⌐ ⌐ ⌐ ⌐ ⌐ ⌐ ⌐ ⌐ ⌐ ⌐ ⌐

The purpose of showing you all of this is to give you an idea of what the computer needs from us in order to operate. However, as you can imagine, writing software by typing in a bunch of zeros and ones (binary) or even a bunch of numbers and letters (hexadecimal) can be excruciatingly painful. Luckily, some very smart guys came up with a programming language called "Assembly" which allows us to write applications using human words such as add, call, and push. These words (also known as "mnemonics") are then translated back into machine code by programs called "assemblers", hence the name "Assembly".

0x03 Intro to the Assembly Programming Language

If you know anything about programming - which I am hoping you do since you are choosing to read this book, you will know that Assembly language programming is as close to machine language programming as you can get. Because of this, software written in Assembly can be developed more efficiently and better optimized than in any other language. However, Assembly-written applications do not have the high-level conveniences such as functions and variables that other programming languages provide which makes developing in Assembly a little more difficult than in other languages (until you know what you are doing). But, it is still much easier and faster than writing a bunch of 1's and 0's.

Even though it is possible to create our own Assembly language syntax, there are two main syntaxes that people tend to use: Intel syntax and AT&T syntax. Identifying one of these syntaxes from the other is quite easy as the AT&T syntax prefixes the $ and % symbols to almost everything. If you have ever done any program disassembly on Linux, you will know that most disassemblers like to use the AT&T syntax by default. But, in my opinion, the Intel syntax is a little cleaner and will therefore be the syntax I use for the examples in this book.

So, how does Assembly work? The Assembly programming language works by using symbols, also called "mnemonics", to represent binary code in a way that humans can easily read and understand it. For example, the following code is a mnemonic way of telling the computer to move the data "0x1234" into the **EAX** register. Depending on the lines that follow this instruction, the computer will do something different with that data from the **BX** register.

MOV EAX, 0x1234

Now, isn't that a lot easier to read than 1011 1000 0011 0100 0001 0010 0000 0000 0000 0000? By the way, Assembly instructions are not case-sensitive. For example, the same line above can also be illustrated as:

mov eax, 0x1234

Also, instead of using hexadecimal values like above, you can also use decimal and even ascii values like this:

mov eax, 4660

With only a few exceptions, Assembly commands come in the form of **MNEMONIC [space] DESTINATION [comma] SOURCE**. If you can remember this simple rule, following Assembly code can actually be quite simple. The only thing you really have left to do from there is learn what each of the mnemonics are and what they do.

Note: We can also add comments (non-instructional messages) to our code by pre-fixing them with a semi-colon like this:

mov eax, 4660 ; Move the value 4660 into the eax register

Since we will be designing our super-cool operating system for the x86 architecture, we can find a full list of x86 mnemonics and instructions at https://en.wikipedia.org/wiki/X86_instruction_listings. For now, I will go ahead and mention some of the most common instructions – at least those that we will be using in our operating system. But before I do that, let's first take a look at how the x86 registers are laid out so that we can have a better idea of what the data looks like as it moves around in the CPU.

As you can see in the diagram below, x86 processors consist of 32-bit general purpose registers. You can think of registers as variables, but in the processor instead of in memory. Since registers are already in the processor and that is where the work actually takes place, using registers instead of memory to store values makes the entire process faster and cleaner.

As shown in the diagram above, the x86 architecture consists of four general purpose registers (EAX, EBX, ECX, and EDX) which are 32-bits. These can then be broken down further into 16-bits (AX, BX, CX, & DX) and even further into 8-bits (AH, AL, BH, BL, CH, CL, DH, & DL). The "H" and "L" suffix on the 8-bit registers represent high and low byte values. (Remember earlier how high and low meant on and off, respectively?)

Everything that includes an "A" (EAX, AX, AH, & AL) are referred to as "accumulator registers". These are used for I/O (input/output), arithmetic, interrupt calls, etc. Everything that includes a "B" (EBX, BX, BH, & BL) are known as "base registers" which are used as base pointers for memory access. Everything with a "C" in it (ECX, CX, CH, & CL) are known as "counter registers". These are used as loop counters and for shifts. Everything with a "D" in it (EDX, DX, DH, & DL) are called "data registers". Similar to the accumulator register, these are used for I/O port access, arithmetic, and some interrupt calls.

The bottom four rows in the diagram above represent indexes (ESI & EDI) and pointers (ESP & EBP). These registers are responsible for pointing to memory addresses where other code is stored and referenced.

17

Going back to the **mov eax, 0x1234 (mov eax, 4660)** example presented earlier, the "**mov**" instruction simply copies data from one location to another. In this case, it moves the value contained in location "4660" into the "**eax**" register. You can also use the "**mov**" instruction to move data from one register to another like so:

mov eax, ebx

In this case, the four bytes of data that are currently at the address contained in the **ebx** register will be moved into the **eax** register. Likewise, you can also use 32-bit constant variables in place of registers. For example, if you wanted to move the contents of **ebx** into the four bytes at memory address "**var**", you would use:

mov [var], ebx

Before we can use our "**var**" (aka "**var**iable"), we will first need to define it. We can do this in a static data region rightfully named "**.data**". Any static data should be declared in the **.data** region which in effect will make it globally available to the rest of our Assembly code. So, before using "**var**" from the example above, we will begin by declaring our **.data** region followed by declaring our variable like so:

.data
var db 32

In this example, we are declaring a variable called "**var**" which will be initialized with the value "32". However, there will be a lot of times where we will not have or know the value to initialize our variable with. In these instances, we can declare an uninitialized byte with the following:

.data
var db ?

Depending on the size required for our variable, we will need to swap out "**db**" with the size that matches our needs. Here is a simple cheat-sheet for identifying which size type to use.

DB = **D**efine **B**yte: 1 byte = 8 bits
DW = **D**efine **W**ord: 2 bytes = 16 bits
DD = **D**efine **D**ouble Word: 4 bytes = 32 bits

Along with the "**mov**" instruction, the next instruction we need to know about is the "**int**" instruction. This instruction is an **int**errupt which tells the hardware to stop what it is doing and do whatever comes next in our list of instructions.

int 0x80

Next up is the "**push**" instruction. Basically, the push instruction tells the system to place its operand on top of the hardware stack in memory. It begins by first decrementing **esp** by four followed by placing its operand into the contents of the 32-bit location at address **esp** (the stack pointer). Since the **esp** instruction is decremented every time the push instruction is performed, the stack grows from high addresses to lower addresses.

Note: "Stack" refers to the simple data structure used in computing for allocating and aligning code so that it can be accessed in a uniform way. As new objects are introduced to the stack, they are placed one on top of the other where the most recent piece of code placed (pushed) onto the stack is the first to be removed (popped) from the stack once it is no longer needed. This is known as Last-In-First-Off (LIFO) since objects further down the stack cannot be accessed or removed from the stack until higher up objects have first been removed.

push eax

If the "**push**" instruction pushes operands onto the stack, how do we get them back off? Well, that is where the "**pop**" instruction comes into play. It works by removing the four bytes data element from the top of the hardware stack (**esp**), moving it into the memory location at **sp**, and then increments **sp** by four.

pop ebx

Aside from the instructions already mentioned, you should also go ahead and learn arithmetic and logic instructions for **add** (**add**ition), **sub** (**sub**traction), **inc** (**inc**rement), **dec** (**dec**rement), **and, or, xor,** and **not**. Also, you should probably go ahead and learn the **jmp** and **call** instructions while you are at it too. Basically, the **jmp** instruction transfers program control flow to the instruction at the memory location indicated by the operand while the **call** instruction calls out to another subroutine (such as in the C code of our kernel which we will learn about in the next chapter).

As mentioned earlier, any time you want to declare global variables, you will need to define them in a section called "**.data**". Similarly, any time you want to perform operations, you will need to define them in a section called "**.text**". However, unlike the .data section which can be written to as well as read, the .text section is read-only. Since the **.text** section is read-only and will never change, this section is loaded into memory only once which reduces the usage and launch time of the application. Even though values in the **.data** section are intended to be changed, you can also use this section to declare constant values that do not change such as file names and buffer sizes.

With that said, there is also a third section called the "**.bss**" section which is used for declaring variables. Wait a minute! I thought the **.data** section was used for declaring variables? Even though you declare variables in the **.data** section, in a "formal" application, the **.data** section will be used for declaring initialized data and constants while the **.bss** section is used for declaring variables that will change during runtime. However, as you will see in the following example, you do not have to include the **.bss** section if you don't need/want it. Just to complicate things even further, when we finally move into building our operating system, we will see that we can also use the **.bss** and not the **.data** section. Although they can be interchangeable, both have their time and place and should be used accordingly for best performance and practice.

To give us our first taste of an Assembly-written application, let's take a look at the series of numbers from the last chapter to see how those decimal, hexadecimal, and binary commands would appear in Assembly.

The instructions for writing, compiling, and executing this code can be found at the end of this book. But for now, I want to briefly explain it as it can help us get a better idea of how the Assembly programming language looks.

print_lucus.asm

```
section .text
global _start

_start:
    mov edx,len
    mov ecx,msg
    mov ebx,1
    mov eax,4
    int 0x80

    mov eax,1
    int 0x80

section .data
    msg db 'Lucus', 0xa
    len equ $ - msg
```

In the above example, you will see that the **.text** section begins with two lines: "**global _start**" and "**_start:**". This is what tells the system where the program execution begins. The "**msg**" part at the beginning of the **.data** section is where we define the text ("Lucus" in this case) that we want to print to the screen and that we want to store this text in the "**msg**" variable as mentioned earlier. Also in the **.data** section, we define another variable called "**len**" which stores the length of the text found in our **msg** variable.

Although we will use the **_start:** symbol in the examples in this book, this definition can actually be named something else as it is only specific to the NASM compiler which we will learn about later. The purpose of using **_start:** (or whatever name you choose) is to tell NASM where the entry point to our application is. The linker application (that we will also learn about later on) will then read this symbol and tell the system that this is where it should look for its first instruction. By adding "**global _start**" at the beginning of our app, the "**global**" directive simply tells NASM to load the "**_start**" symbol into the object code so that it can be found later on in this location.

Back in the **.text** section after "**_start:**" (where our program execution begins), we tell the processor to move the value from our **len** variable into the **edx** register followed by moving the actual text itself into the **ecx** register. Basically, this is telling the system to allocate [**len**] bytes so that we can store [**msg**] text in that allocated space.

After that, the "**mov ebx, 1**" command indicates "standard output" (aka "print to terminal") while "**move eax, 4**" is a system call to "sys_write". Immediately after those commands you will see "**int 0x80**" (again, "**int**" is short for "**int**errupt") which passes control over to the kernel, allowing for any system calls to be made ("write to standard output" in this case). The "**move eax, 1**" command is a system call to "sys_exit" which tells the system that it has completed and that the following "**int 0x80**" should once again return control back over to the kernel for whatever processing is next on the stack (or to exit since there are no more instructions).

⌐ ⌐ ⌐ ⌐ ⌐ ⌐ ⌐ ⌐ ⌐ ⌐ ⌐ ⌐ ⌐ ⌐ ⌐

At this point, you should have a very simple Assembly application that prints "Lucus" (or whatever text you chose to use) to the terminal. Based on this simple application, you should also have a very basic understanding of how the Assembly programming language works. It isn't much, but it is enough to get you started with creating your own operating system. With that said, if you found the Assembly programming language a little difficult to follow, don't worry. The next chapter will show you something that makes programming a computer a little easier than if it was all done in Assembly.

0x04 Intro to the C Programming Language

There are plenty of books and other resources for learning the C programming language and I encourage you to look into those to further advance your skills. But, I still want to take some time to introduce you to the basics required to get started developing in the C programming language since it is what we will be using to develop the majority of our operating system.

As we learned in the last chapter, the Assembly programming language is just an abstraction from machine code. Even though Assembly can make programming easier, it is still a little difficult to learn and follow. To help with that, between 1969 and 1973, a man at AT&T Bell Labs named Dennis M. Ritchie brought us yet another abstraction layer on top of machine instructions called the C programming language.

According to Wikipedia, *"C is a general-purpose, imperative computer programming language, supporting structured programming, lexical variable scope and recursion, while a static type system prevents many unintended operations. By design, C provides constructs that map efficiently to typical machine instructions, and therefore it has a found lasting use in applications that had formerly been coded in Assembly language, including operating systems, as well as various application software for computers ranging from supercomputers to embedded systems."*

I know that is a mouthful, but let me break it down for you. Basically, C is a high-level programming language (where machine code / binary is the low-level language) that allows you to read and write code for a large number of platforms. Not only does C allow you to develop applications for pretty much any kind of system you can imagine, but it also allows you to develop applications that are optimized to perform at the fastest speeds possible. This is because applications written in C get compiled straight to machine instructions, just like with applications written in Assembly but not quite as fast. If application speed is what matters, you should stick with developing everything in Assembly. But, if you can afford to trade-off a slight performance hit for easier development, then you will not be disappointed with C.

It is also worth noting that C was originally invented as a way to develop the UNIX operating system. Since we too are wanting to create our own operating system, you can see why C is an obvious choice for us to program in. Not to mention, once you get the hang of the C programming language, you can continue to use it to further develop your operating system as well as have a nice employable skill in your toolbox.

So, how does the C programming language work? Well, to begin with, the C programming language is based on the premise of providing a list of procedures - also known as routines, subroutines, or functions - that the computer must follow. Inside each procedure is a list of instructions, similar to those found in Assembly, that when followed enable the computer to do the many things a computer is capable of. In Assembly, these procedures are listed in what we learned in the last chapter as "sections". Sections in Assembly are declared by the word "section" followed by a period prefixed to its name.

section .text

In C, these sections are called "procedures" which is why developing applications in the C programming language is known as "procedural programming" which is derived from "structured programming". Each procedure consists of the procedure's return type followed by the procedure name followed by a list of parameters that are expected to be passed into the procedure which are all contained within parenthesis.

int say_hello (char *to)

The most common procedure, that also happens to be found in all C applications, is the "main" procedure. This procedure is required in all C applications because it is the entry point for all applications. In fact, the *main* procedure has a one-to-one mapping to the _start: symbol found in Assembly like we learned about in the last chapter. The purpose of the *main* procedure is to kick off the list of instructions that the system must follow and, in return, notify the system whether or not the application started successfully.

In order to do this in a common fashion, all *main* procedures are required to return a zero or a non-zero integer: zero meaning success, non-zero meaning failure where each non-zero response can mean something different. As mentioned before, all procedures are declared first with its return type followed by its name and a list of parameters contained within parenthesis. The return type simply tells the system what type of value to expect it to send back upon completion. After the parenthesis, procedures include beginning and ending curly braces (i.e. **{** and **}**) which wrap the procedure's list of instructions.

The best way to explain the "main" procedure would be to see an example of it. The following example is the C representation of the example from the last chapter that prints my name, "Lucus", to the screen.

print_lucus.c

```
int main() {
    puts("Lucus");
    return 0;
}
```

Since the *main* procedure is required to return either a zero or a non-zero integer to indicate success or failure respectively, we define the procedure as "**int**" (short for "**int**eger"). As you will notice in the example above, the very last thing we do is return a zero which indicates everything has executed as expected. If we wanted to indicate that something went awry, we could simply return something such as one or negative one.

You will also notice in the example above that the parentheses do not include any parameters as stated earlier. This is because, in the *main* procedure, it is implied that it will always contain "int argc" and "char *argv[]" as its parameters. The purpose of these parameters is to allow users to pass in parameters to our application from the command line. For example, if instead of hardcoding my name, "Lucus", in the example above, we choose to allow users to pass in a name when running the app from the command line, we would need to include these parameters like so:

```
int main(int argc, char *argv[]) {
   ....
}
```

Note: If we do not use those parameters within our application, there is no need to define them in the procedure.

The first parameter, "**int argc**", is an integer that indicates the **arg**ument **c**ount. This tells the application how many parameters it should be expecting. The second parameter, "**char *argv[]**" is a string representation of the parameters you are passing into the application. The "**argv**" name is short for **arg**ument **v**ector. As you can see, the [] brackets after "**argv**" indicate that this is an array. This array will always contain the application name as its first value and all remaining arguments will make up the remainder of the array.

The "**puts**" instruction in the example above is what tells the system to output "Lucus" to the console. Later on we will use the "**puts**" function in our operating system as well as a similar function called "**printf**". One difference between **puts** and **printf** is that the former always appends a new-line character ("\n") to the end of whatever is to be printed. If we want the **printf** function to print a new-line, we will need to include "\n" along with our string as shown below.

printf("Lucus\n");

Even though the line above shows how to use the **printf** function with a new-line, I would highly recommend that you do not use this function in the manner demonstrated above when only printing a variable (more on that in a minute). For now, the second difference between **puts** and **printf** is that the latter is used to interpret arguments as formatted strings. Whereas the **puts** function only accepts one argument and outputs that straight to the screen, the **printf** function can accept a string-literal as its first argument followed by as many arguments as needed to match the number of format parameters found within the first string-literal argument.

Format parameters are simply placeholders that get replaced by their counterparts in the subsequent arguments that get passed to the **printf** function. Format parameters are denoted by the percentage sign (%) followed by a character that tells the **printf** function how to interpret its argument. The format parameters that we will be using in our operating system are %c (single character) and %s (string of characters). Here is a list of the most common format parameters supported by the **printf** function.

%c	single character
%d or %i	signed decimal integer
%e	scientific notation (mantissa/exponent) using e character
%E	scientific notation (mantissa/exponent) using E character
%f	decimal floating point
%g	uses the shorter of %e or %f
%G	uses the shorter of %E or %f
%o	signed octal
%s	string of characters
%u	unsigned decimal integer
%x	unsigned hexadecimal integer
%X	unsigned hexadecimal integer (capital letters)
%p	pointer address
%n	nothing printed

Here are a couple of examples of using the **printf** function.

```
printf(string);
printf("Lucus\n");
printf("Name: %s", "Lucus");
printf("Name: %s", string);
```

In order to use the **printf** procedure, you will first need to add a reference to a file that knows about this procedure. To do that, you will add a line that includes a ".h" file called "**stdio.h**" so that you can use any functions that **stdio.h** knows about. These ".h" files are known as "**header**" files which are nothing more than files that contain definitions of functions/procedures found in other ".c" files. Here is what our code would look like if we were to replace the **puts** call with a call to **printf**.

print_lucus.c

```
#include <stdio.h>
int main(int argc, char *argv[]) {
    printf("Number of arguments: %d, Name: %s\n", argc, argv[1]);
    return 0;
}
```

If passing in "Lucus" as your only argument, the above example will output the following:

output

```
Number of arguments: 2, Name: Lucus
```

Again, we will get two as the number of arguments because the application name itself will always be stored as the first value in the **argv** array. If we want to print the application name instead of the second argument being passed in, we can simply replace **argv[1]** with **argv[0]** in the example above.

When using the **#include** statement, you will notice that sometimes the file names are wrapped with < and > symbols while other times file names are wrapped with double-quotes. Any time you see an include wrapped with < and >, it means that the compiler should look for the library version of the file first. If it cannot locate the library version of the file, the compiler will then look in the local directory for the file. Any time you see an include wrapped with double-quotes, it means the compiler should look in the local directory first. If it cannot locate the file in the local directory, it should then look for it in the library location instead.

Since our applications can grow quite large, especially is the case when developing our own operating system, it is recommended that we move procedures into their own .c files and list their definitions (procedure return type, name, and parameters list) in their own .h files and reference those files from other files. Not only does this help minimize the amount of code in any given file which makes it easier to follow, but it also helps us to develop reusable code that can be called from any other application later down the road as well. Plus, every time we have code in our application and run said application, every bit of code included in our application will get loaded into memory whether that code gets executed or not. So, by having our procedures in their own .h and .c files and only calling those procedures only when/if needed, we can reduce the amount of memory required for executing our application which can also provide our app with better performance in regards to its speed of execution.

As mentioned earlier, it is bad practice to use the first example above to print values from variables using the **printf** procedure and not including a format string (i.e. **printf(string);**). Even though it will work functionally, it can lead to security vulnerabilities in our application. You can find lots of information online about this vulnerability by searching for *"format string vulnerability in printf"*. You can also contact me directly if you would like to learn more about it as I have personally found and exploited this vulnerability in several applications I have been responsible for throughout my career.

Once we have written our C code, we will need to compile it before we can run it. To do that with the examples and operating system illustrated in this book, we will use the "gcc" compiler that we will learn to install in the next chapter. For now, the only thing we really need to know is that we compile applications by going to the command prompt and typing "gcc" followed by the name of your .c file like so:

gcc print_lucus.c

If we run the command above, gcc will compile our code and output a file called "**a.out**" which we can execute with the following command:

./a.out

If you prefer to use a different name for your compiled application output, you can declare it by using the "**-o**" flag followed by the name you want to use. For example, if I want to compile the print_lucus.c example from above and output it to an executable file called "**runme**", I would use the following command:

gcc print_lucus.c **-o runme**

Then, I could execute the application with the following:

./runme

As explained before, the **main** procedure is expected to return an integer. Therefore, we begin our procedure declaration with "**int**" (short for **int**eger). Other procedures will have the need to return other types such as a character, strings of characters, and so on. For those, we will need to declare our procedure with the appropriate return type. However, there will also be lots of times where we want to execute a procedure that isn't expected to return anything at all. For these, we will use "**void**" at the beginning of our procedure declaration. For example, if we want to create a procedure that uses the **printf** function and can be reused from multiple locations throughout our operating system, we could create a new procedure like so:

```
void print_name(char *name) {
    printf("Name: %s\n", name);
}
```

We can then call this procedure from any other procedure. For example, if we want to call this procedure from our **main** procedure, our code would look like the following.

print_lucus.c
```
#include <stdio.h>

void print_name(char *name) {
    printf("Name: %s\n", name);
}
```

```
int main(int argc, char *argv[]) {
    print_name(argv[1]);
    return 0;
}
```

Whenever the system loads our application into memory and the CPU so that it can be executed, procedures (and everything else) are loaded onto what is called the "**stack**". As things get loaded, whatever is encountered first in the code gets placed onto the stack first. The next piece of code that is encountered gets loaded on top of that and so on. Because of this and because the **main** procedure depends on the **print_name** procedure in the example above, we have to make sure that **print_name** is already available on the stack so that it can be called from **main**. To make sure that happens, we will need to make sure that **print_name** is listed in our code above the place it gets called later on (i.e. in the **main** procedure). Basically, the rule of thumb is that any time we plan on calling another piece of code, that other piece of code needs to be defined in our application above the line of code that calls it. This is why you will always find **#include** statements at the top of any application. Other programming languages such as Java and C# take care of arranging code on the stack for you.

Back to our "**void**" example, many programmers believe that **void** has no meaning in applications. Unfortunately for them, they are wrong. The "**void**" keyword is a pointer and can be used as a pointer either to procedures or to variables. The **void** pointer's main purpose is to simply hold a memory address. Otherwise, if "**void**" had no meaning, the system would not know about the code found in that memory location and therefore would not do anything with it. For the examples and purposes found in this book, we only need to know that **void** procedures are not expected to return anything. But, I still thought I would mention the part about **void** pointers holding memory addresses to help with your knowledge of how computers work.

In this chapter I introduced you to the C programming language where we learned the basic structure of C code, how to reference code in external files, and how to pass parameters to applications and other procedures. By now you should have a pretty good grasp of what it takes to write and compile an application in C. Now it is time to put together an environment that will allow us to do all of this and to move us one step closer to having our own operating system.

0x05 Getting Started

In order for us to develop an operating system, we will first need an operating system that provides all of the tools necessary for building our new operating system. Lucky for us, there are already plenty of options for us to choose from. Even though OS development can be done in Windows, we will use Linux for our development and for the exercises in this book. To be specific, we will be using **CentOS** (**C**ommunity **ENT**erprise **O**perating **S**ystem) which you can get from https://www.centos.org. However, instead of replacing our current installation of Windows with Linux, we will instead use a virtualized environment where we will not only run Linux, but where we will also test our new operating system.

One of the best things about running a VM (Virtual Machine) is that whenever we need to shut down our computer, we don't have to also power down the operating system running in the VM. Instead, we can simply save the current state of our VM and close it so that the next time we open our VM, everything is exactly where we left it.

Another great thing about running a VM is that should we do anything that damages the operating system in the VM, we do not run the same risk of damaging our host operating system (the one that is running the physical computer). If we do run into any issues, we can always start from scratch and rebuild everything again. Or, more preferably, we can simply delete the current VM and replace it with a backup or "snapshot" that we make periodically when working within our VM environment.

Installing Virtualbox

For our virtualization environment, we will be using a product called **VirtualBox**. According to their website (https://www.virtualboxorg), *"VirtualBox is a powerful x86 and AMD64/Intel64 virtualization product for enterprise as well as home use. Not only is VirtualBox an extremely feature rich, high performance product for enterprise customers, it is also the only professional solution that is freely available as Open Source Software under the terms of the GNU General Public License (GPL) verion 2."*

If you have never worked with a virtualized environment before, the basic idea is that you can run multiple operating systems on your computer from within your current operating system and without replacing or interfering with your current OS or file system. For example, throughout this book I will be assuming that you are running Windows as the primary operating system on your computer. But, instead of replacing Windows with Linux or doing anything that will mess up our Windows installation, we will run Linux from inside of Windows as if it is just another application such as Word or Excel.

To get started, we will open our browser and navigate to https://www.virtualbox.org/wiki/Downloads.

There we will find links to download VirtualBox for Windows hosts, OS X hosts, Linux hosts, and Solaris hosts. Since I am assuming you are running Windows as mentioned before, we will need to download the version for "Windows hosts" which is (as of the writing of this book) version 5.0.10.

After we have downloaded VirtualBox, we will run it to begin the installation process. Unless you have other reasons not to, you should stick with the default options that the installer suggests. Toward the end of the installation, you will be presented with a warning message that reads, *"Installing the Oracle VM VirtualBox 5.0.10 Networking feature will reset your network connection and temporarily disconnect you from the network."* This is OK. Just click the "Yes" button followed by clicking the "Install" button on the next screen to install VirtualBox. Depending on your system settings, you may be asked throughout the installation process to approve the installation of the various components.

Installing Linux

Now that we have a place to run Linux, we will need to download Linux itself. To do that, we will open our browser and navigate to https://www.centos.org/download/.

There we will find links to download a "DVD ISO", "Everything ISO", or a "Minimal ISO". You can choose any of the ISO's you want. But for the purposes of this book, you should choose to download the "Minimal ISO". If you would prefer to boot your computer into Linux and not run Linux from inside of Windows using VirtualBox as explained in this book, you can choose to download the "DVD ISO" and burn it to a DVD (or thumbdrive), but you will need to locate instructions for doing that on your own. For now, just stick with downloading the "Minimal ISO".

Once CentOS has finished downloading, open VirtualBox and click the "New" button in the upper-left corner. This will open a modal window that will ask you about the virtual machine you are attempting to create. For the "Name" field, type in something meaningful such as "CentOS" or similar so that you can easily identify your development environment OS from other virtualized operating systems, including the OS you are about to build.

Next, click on the "Type" dropdown and select "Linux" for the type followed by "Red Hat (64-bit)" for the Version. Now, I'm sure you are probably asking yourself, "Why am I selecting Red Hat when I downloaded CentOS?" Well, that is because CentOS and Red Hat are almost identical with a few exceptions that we don't need to concern ourselves with for the purposes of this book. And, to be honest, I don't think it really matters what you select for the Version since we will be loading CentOS anyways.

Since this will be our development environment, it is recommended to select as much memory for our Virtual Machine (VM) as possible. Just remember that we will be running Linux and Windows (and our new OS) at the same time. So, we will need to make sure that all systems are allocated enough memory so that the computer doesn't begin performing slowly. But, your memory size selection will all be dependent on how much physical memory your computer has. To give you a starting idea, the laptop I am using has 32GB of RAM. So, selecting 8GB (8192MB) is plenty for running my CentOS development environment without compromising the Windows host. For the Hard Disk, choose the second option - "Create a virtual hard disk now" - and click the "Create" button.

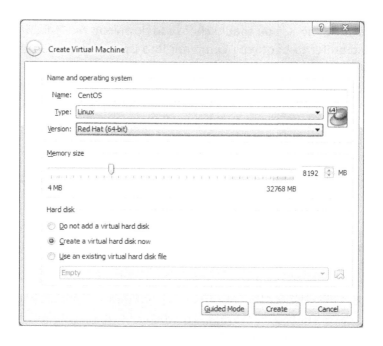

On the next screen, we will need to choose a location on our file system where we want to store the VM we are currently creating. Before we select a File Location, we will need to select "VHD (Virtual Hard disk)" for the "Hard disk file type". Then, we will click the icon to the right of the File Location field to select where we want to create and save this file. Since most computers now come with a fairly decent amount of disk space, you can set the File Size to whatever makes sense for you. If you aren't planning on doing a whole lot more with your CentOS development environment aside from creating your new / cool operating system, you can stick with the proposed 8GB. However, if you plan on cross-compiling your OS to run on other architectures (such as on the Raspberry Pi as shown in Chapter 12), you will need to specify a larger file size. As shown below, I chose to go with 16GB since the cross-compiler from Chapter 12 requires an additional 3.5GB. Plus, if I decide to create other cross-compilers, those too will require more space as well. When you are done, click the "Create" button to create the VM and close the modal window.

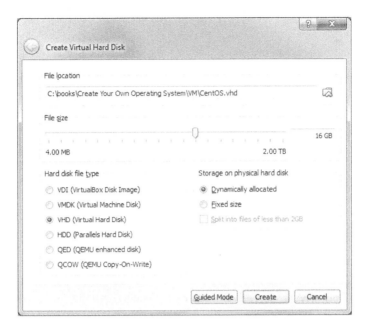

At this point we should see "CentOS" (or whatever we named our development environment) in the VirtualBox list on the left. Go ahead and click to select CentOS from the list on the left and click the "Start" button from the toolbar. This will launch the VM where the first thing we will be asked is to select a start-up disk. To do that, click the folder icon with the green arrow, change directories to the location where you downloaded the CentOS ISO and select it.

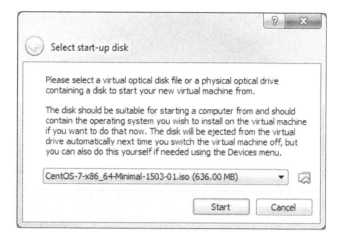

With our ISO selected, we will click the "Start" button to proceed.

As soon as our VM is started, we will click inside the VM to take control of it. Using your arrow keys, move up to select "Install CentOS" and press the enter key. At this point, you will be asked to provide input in the form of a wizard for selecting things such as your language and dialect of choice, date & time, keyboard, etc... You will also be asked to select an installation destination. To do that, click on the "INSTALLATION DESTINATION" option under "SYSTEM". VirtualBox will select the first and only drive in the list. If you have a need for an additional disk, go for it. Otherwise, just click the "Done" button in the upper-left corner to select the only drive you have for your VM and return to the previous screen.

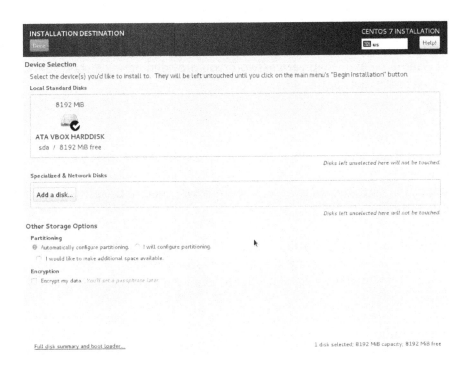

When you are ready to move on, click the "Begin Installation" button in the lower-right corner and you will be taken to a screen that not only begins the installation process, but it also asks you to create a root password and a secondary user. You will need to provide a password for root *and* create a secondary user before completing the installation process. Just make sure you provide something you will remember. If you use something weak for your password (such as "root"), you will need to press the "Done" button in the upper-left corner twice to confirm it as indicated by the yellow bar at the bottom of your screen. Make sure you also create a secondary user at this time as we will be using that user for the exercises remaining in this book.

While CentOS is being installed, press the Ctrl key to the right of your spacebar to release the mouse from the VM and give control back to Windows until the installation has completed. When the installation has finished, click back inside your VM to move your mouse control back to it and press the "Finish configuration" button in the bottom-right corner.

Afterwards, you will need to click the "Reboot" button to restart CentOS at which point you will be dropped into a login prompt where you will enter the username and whatever password you provided during installation. Do not log in as "root" at this time.

Installing GNOME

In order to do some development, there are several tools that we will need to install. Before we can do that, we will first need to configure our network connection since the tools we will be using will need to be fetched directly from the web.

There are a few ways to do this. But, thankfully CentOS provides a very simple mechanism for configuring our network connection. At the command prompt, type the following command to open the Network Manager in GUI Mode.

sudo nmtui

Note: Do not type the leading # sign. It is only there to indicate that this command is to be entered at the console prompt.

Next, press the enter key to select "Edit a connection". More than likely you should only have one network interface available in the list on the next screen. Regardless, use your arrow keys to select the network interface you will be using and press the enter key to choose it.

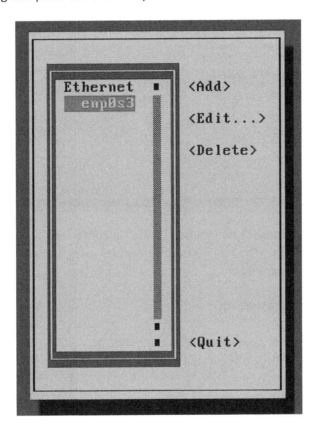

Since you probably don't care how VirtualBox connects to your host computer for accessing the Internet, you can leave "IPv4 CONFIGURATION" set to "Automatic" and will need to check "Automatically connect" in order to enable DHCP. To check the box next to "Automatically connect", use your arrow keys to navigate down until it turns red. Then, press the spacebar to select it. After that, use the arrow keys again to navigate to "OK" and press the enter key to return to the network interface selection screen. Move the cursor down to "Quit" so that it is red. Then, simply press the enter key to quit the Network Manager.

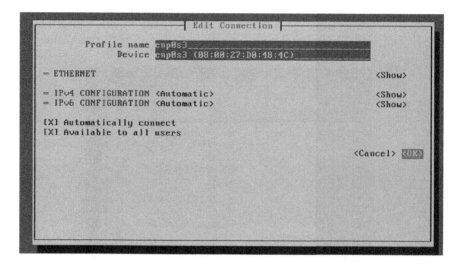

Now that your network connection has been configured, it is time to make CentOS aware of it. You can do that by restarting the network service using the following command:

sudo systemctl restart network

You can verify that your network connection is working by executing the following command which should result in some results and no errors.

ping google.com

```
[root@localhost ~]# systemctl restart network
[root@localhost ~]# ping google.com
PING google.com (74.125.138.101) 56(84) bytes of data.
64 bytes from 74.125.138.101: icmp_seq=1 ttl=43 time=14.2 ms
64 bytes from 74.125.138.101: icmp_seq=2 ttl=43 time=13.5 ms
64 bytes from 74.125.138.101: icmp_seq=3 ttl=43 time=14.3 ms
^C
--- google.com ping statistics ---
3 packets transmitted, 3 received, 0% packet loss, time 2002ms
rtt min/avg/max/mdev = 13.525/14.045/14.325/0.368 ms
[root@localhost ~]# _
```

Press Ctrl+C to stop pinging the Google servers and to drop you back to the prompt.

Even though it is possible to do all of your OS development from the console, I find it easier to do development from a GUI (Graphical User Interface) environment. There are a few options to choose from when selecting a GUI. But, for the exercises in this book, I will be working with and referring to the GNOME Desktop Environment which you can install by executing the following command:

sudo yum -y groupinstall "GNOME Desktop"

Depending on your Internet connection speed, it will probably take a little while for GNOME to install. For me, it took about three minutes to download everything and about an hour to install it all. So, go have yourself a coffee & a sandwich and check back later. When you return, your screen will probably be black. If it is, simply click inside the VM and press one of the arrow keys. You should now see your screen again. If everything is still installing, you can press the Ctrl key to the right of your spacebar just like before to return control back to Windows where you can do other things while the installation finishes.

After the installation has completed and you are back to a command prompt, type the following command to start the GNOME desktop.

startx

Every time you reboot CentOS, you will need to run "startx" to get back into the GNOME desktop. However, if you want to have GNOME automatically load every time you restart, you can do that using "targets" (instead of "runlevels" from previous versions). The following commands will tell CentOS to load the GNOME GUI on system start from now on.

sudo rm /etc/systemd/system/default.target
sudo ln -sf /lib/systemd/system/graphical.target
/etc/systemd/system/default.target

Note: The last two lines above should be executed as a single line (i.e., there is no line break between "graphical.target" and "/etc/systemd".

When GNOME loads up for the very first time, you will be presented with the Gnome-initial-setup where you will be asked to select your language of choice, input sources, and whether you want to "connect to your existing data in the cloud". After you click the "Start using CentOS Linux" button at the end of the setup, you will be ready to load the tools needed for building your own operating system.

Preparing CentOS and the VM

Before we move on, it is recommended that we update CentOS so that everything from this point on works as expected. To do that from inside of GNOME, click on **Applications > Utilities > Terminal**, then run the following command to update your entire system.

sudo yum -y update

Note: This will probably take several minutes to run. For me, it took around thirty minutes to complete.

Next, we will need to install the VirtualBox Guest Additions which will allow us to do things later on such as dragging and dropping files between our Windows host and CentOS guest as well as copying and pasting text between the two. To do that, the first thing we will need to do is execute the following commands to install the kernel development tools that will be needed by the guest additions installer.

```
# sudo yum -y install gcc kernel-devel
# echo export KERN_DIR=/usr/src/kernels/`uname -r` >> ~/.bashrc
# reboot
```

After CentOS has restarted, we will need to install the VirtualBox Guest Additions by clicking Devices on the VM menu bar and selecting "Insert Guest Additions CD image..." Inside the VM, you should see a message confirming that you trust the VBOXADDITIONS CD. Go ahead and click the "Run" button to confirm this.

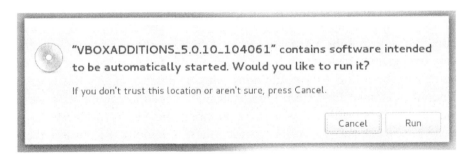

Once Guest Additions have been installed, you will see a message telling you everything was successful and that you now need to restart the guest system (CentOS). It is a good idea that you also restart Windows at this point too (just in case).

```
                    VirtualBox Guest Additions installation

 File  Edit  View  Search  Terminal  Help
Verifying archive integrity... All good.
Uncompressing VirtualBox 5.0.10 Guest Additions for Linux...........
VirtualBox Guest Additions installer
Removing installed version 5.0.10 of VirtualBox Guest Additions...
Removing existing VirtualBox non-DKMS kernel modules[  OK  ]
Copying additional installer modules ...
Installing additional modules ...
Removing existing VirtualBox non-DKMS kernel modules[  OK  ]
Building the VirtualBox Guest Additions kernel modules
Building the main Guest Additions module[  OK  ]
Building the shared folder support module[  OK  ]
Building the OpenGL support module[  OK  ]
Doing non-kernel setup of the Guest Additions[  OK  ]
Starting the VirtualBox Guest Additions [  OK  ]
Installing the Window System drivers
Installing X.Org Server 1.15 modules[  OK  ]
Setting up the Window System to use the Guest Additions[  OK  ]
You may need to restart the the Window System (or just restart the guest system)
to enable the Guest Additions.

Installing graphics libraries and desktop services components[  OK  ]
Press Return to close this window...
```

Troubleshooting VirtualBox Guest Additions

For some reason, you might experience times when you can no longer drag/drop or copy/paste between your CentOS guest machine and your Windows host machine. When this happens, you can usually redo the steps above to re-install the VirtualBox Guest Additions and everything will start working again. However, I have experienced times when CentOS will complain about the Guest Additions with a message along the lines of "mount: unknown filesystem type 'iso9660'". If you encounter this, don't worry. There is a manual way of remounting the VBOXADDITIONS CD in CentOS so that you can re-install the Guest Additions. Below are those steps.

sudo mkdir /media/VirtualBoxGuestAdditions/
sudo mount /dev/cdrom /media/VirtualBoxGuestAdditions

You should get the following error at this point:

> mount: unknown filesystem type 'iso9660'

ls /lib/modules/
Make note of the "generic" folder with the highest version number here.

insmod /lib/modules/*[replace me with the version number above]*-generic/kernel/fs/isofs/isofs.ko
sudo mount /dev/cdrom /media/VirtualBoxGuestAdditions
> mount: block device /dev/sr0 is write-protected, mounting read-only
sudo /media/VirtualBoxGuestAdditions/VBoxLinuxAdditions.run

Preparing the Development Environment

At the beginning of this chapter, we downloaded and installed the minimal version of the CentOS ISO. Because of that, there are a few development tools missing that we will now need to install.

The first is the GNU Compiler Collection also known as "**gcc**". This is the tool that we will be using to compile our C code into machine code. We're also installing g++ (via "gcc-c++") now since we'll be needing it later on for our cross-compiler.

Since we are focusing (for now) on compiling our OS to run on the x86 architecture, the next tool we will need to install is the **Netwide Assembler** also known as "**nasm**". This is the tool we will use to compile our Assembly code into machine code.

The third tool we will need to install is called "**tk**" which is a graphical toolkit for the Tcl scripting language. This is needed by one of the dependencies needed for building our ISO.

Even though we can install gcc, g++, nasm, and tk separately, we can also knock them all out with a single line. To install them all at the same time, run the following command:

sudo yum -y install gcc nasm tk

When it comes time for us to cross-compile our operating system for other architectures, there are a few other dependencies we will need. So, let's go ahead and install them now.

sudo yum -y install gcc-c++ glibc-devel glibc-static libstdc++* glibc.i686

Next, we will need to manually download and install **xorriso** which is needed by the utility we will be using to create our ISO as mentioned above. You can find the latest version of xorriso on the gnu website at http://www.gnu.org/software/xorriso/#download. Run the following commands to install xorriso. If you download a different version of xorriso, just be sure to swap out "1.4.2" with the appropriate version number found on the gnu website.

wget http://www.gnu.org/software/xorriso/xorriso-1.4.2.tar.gz
tar -zxvf xorriso-1.4.2.tar.gz
cd xorriso-1.4.2/
./configure
make
sudo make install

That's it! We now have all the tools we will need for developing and compiling our very own operating system. But before moving on, there is still one more thing that we can do to make our development a little easier. Later on we will have the need to copy the ISO we will create for our OS from the CentOS VirtualBox VM to our Windows computer where we will create a separate VirtualBox VM for testing it. Plus, there will be times where we will want to copy other files and text between our VirtualBox VM and our host machine.

In order to enable copying and pasting between our VirtualBox VM guest and Windows host, we will first need to power off our CentOS VM. To do that, simply click the X in the upper-right corner and tell it to "Power Off". Once the VM window has closed, select CentOS from the list in the VirtualBox Manager and click Settings on the toolbar. Under the General section, click the Advanced tab and change both "Shared Clipboard" and "Drag 'n Drop" to "Bidirectional" as shown below.

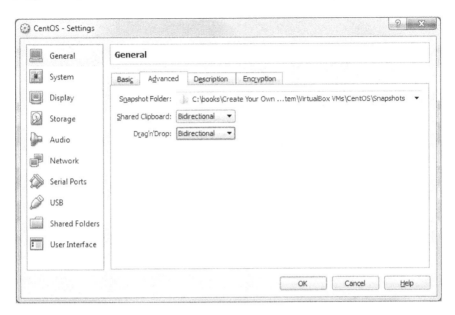

After you have made those changes, click the OK button to return to the VirtualBox Manager. From there, you can restart your CentOS VM by selecting the VM from the list on the left and clicking the Start button. If you ran the "ln -sf" command earlier in the "Installing GNOME" section, CentOS should load you back into the GNOME desktop. If it doesn't, you can return by simply executing the "startx" command.

⌐   ⌐   ⌐   ⌐   ⌐   ⌐   ⌐   ⌐   ⌐   ⌐   ⌐   ⌐   ⌐   ⌐   ⌐

Congratulations! We now have an environment setup that will allow us to develop our very own operating system.

\

0x06 Bootstrapping with the Bootloader

When you power on a computer, the first thing to run is what is known as the "Basic Input Output System" (BIOS). The BIOS is responsible for verifying that all of the hardware has powered on successfully and is ready for use. This test is known as the "Power-On Self-Test" (POST). In most systems that do not pass the POST, a series of beeps are played that – depending on their tone and frequency – indicate what has gone wrong (or right) and why the system has halted (or started). You can do a Google search to find a list of beep-codes that are specific to your platform or you can use the list of codes on Wikipedia found at https://en.wikipedia.org/wiki/Power-on_self-test.

On an x86 system, the CPU is pre-configured to look for the last sixteen bytes of the 32-bit address space (0xFFFFFFF0) for a "jump" instruction to the address in memory where the BIOS has copied itself. When found, the system will kick off the BIOS which will initiate the POST test.

Once all hardware has powered on and the POST has passed successfully, the BIOS will look for the operating system and will turn control over to it if found. The first piece of the OS that gets loaded into memory is known as the "Master Boot Record" (MBR). The MBR is the first sector found on a bootable device and is only 512 bytes in size: 446 bytes for the primary bootloader and 64 bytes for the partition table that describes the primary and extended partitions.

When the BIOS has successfully located the MBR that contains bootable code, it will take this code and load it into memory starting from physical address "0x07c0" at which point the CPU will jump to and execute the code. The code that gets loaded and executed is known as the "bootloader" (short for "bootstrap loader"). If all goes according to plan, the bootloader will then load the kernel into physical address 0x10000000 which loads the rest of the operating system. We will learn about the kernel in the next chapter. The main thing to know here is that the bootloader contains the entry point into our system.

To help us better understand how the bootloader works, we will now take a quick look at a simple bootloader used on x86 architectures. Even though it is possible to use this for bootstrapping our own operating system, we will not be using this bootloader going forward. Instead, we will opt for using already provided bootloaders which we will learn about shortly. For now, let's take a look at the bootloader code.

With your CentOS environment running in VirtualBox and booted into the desktop, click on **Applications > Accessories > gedit** to open the text editor we will be using for writing our code. Then, click on **File > New** (or press Ctrl + N or click the white-paper icon on the toolbar) to open a new / blank file. Type the following code into that new file and save the file as "**bootloader.asm**". You can save the file where ever you want. But for the purposes of this book, we will save our file into a new folder on the Desktop called "**bootloader**".

The following code will boot the system and print a simple "Hello world!" message to the screen one character at a time and then halt the system.

bootloader.asm

```
bits 16

start:
    mov ax, 0x07c0
    add ax, 0x20
    mov ss, ax
    mov sp, 4096

    mov ax, 0x07c0
    mov ds, ax

    mov si, msg
    call print
    cli
    hlt
```

```
data:
    msg db 'Hello world!', 0
print:
    mov ah, 0x0e

.printchar:
    lodsb
    cmp al, 0
    je .done
    int 0x10
    jmp .printchar

.done:
    ret

times 510 - ($ - $$) db 0
dw 0xaa55
```

Since Chapter 3 gave us an introduction to the Assembly programming language and because we will cover it quite extensively in the upcoming section about creating our entry point, I will not go into the details about what the code in this bootloader does. However, one thing I believe *is* worth mentioning in this bootloader code is the fact that it begins with "**bits 16**" which indicates the code is intended to be executed in 16-bit mode as opposed to the 32-bit mode the rest of our operating system will be running in.

The reason for this is because when all x86 architectures boot up, they start out running in what is called "real mode" (where the bootloader runs) and eventually get switched to "protected mode" where everything else gets ran. The main difference between real mode and protected mode is that in real mode, all applications run within the same memory at the same time. Therefore, any running applications can access the memory space of all of the other running applications. As you can imagine, this would create a security nightmare. Therefore, after the bootloader has finished doing its work (loading the system and turning over execution to the kernel), the system then switches into protected mode where applications are physically isolated from each other due to the nature of running in different address spaces.

Even though we will not be using this particular bootloader for our operating system, I at least wanted to provide you with the code so that you would have it in the event you want to create your own bootloader for other projects. And, since we already have the code, we should also take a look at how to compile and test it.

In order for us to test the above bootloader, we will first need to compile it. To do that, open a terminal in your CentOS environment, use the "cd" command to change directory into the location where you saved the **bootloader.asm** file, and execute the following command.

```
# nasm -f bin -o bootloader.img bootloader.asm
```

Within the same folder that contains your **bootloader.asm** file, you should now also see an additional file called "**bootloader.img**". Next, copy the newly created **bootloader.img** file from your CentOS environment over to your Windows environment. Then, inside VirtualBox, go to **Machine > New...** to open the "Create Virtual Machine" dialog. From there, enter something such as "Test Bootloader" for the "Name" field and select "Other" and "Other/Unknown" for the "Type" and "Version". Select "Do not add a virtual hard disk" and click the "Create" button.

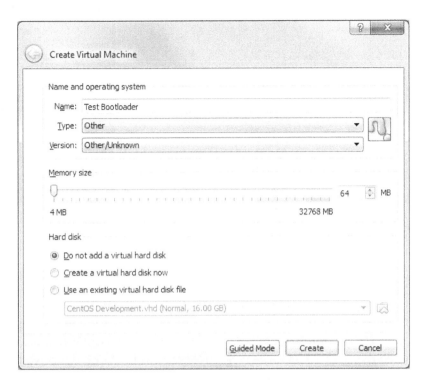

After you click the "Create" button, you should now see a new virtual machine in the list on the left-side of VirtualBox. At this time, we will need to create a bootable drive to run our bootloader from. To do that, select the new VM from the list and click the "Settings" button on the toolbar. Once the settings dialog has appeared, select "Storage" from the list on the left. Next, right-click in the white space under the word "Empty" in the "Storage Tree" and select "Add Floppy Controller". Then, right-click on "Controller: Floppy" from the list and select "Add Floppy Drive". This will pop up a dialog window where you will need to click the "Choose disk" button, navigate to, and select the **bootloader.img** file you copied over from your CentOS environment.

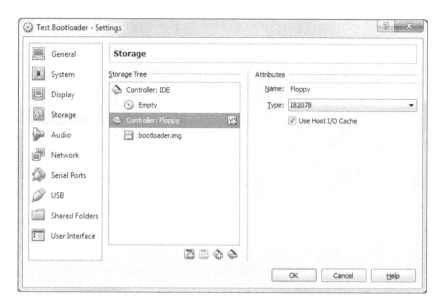

Once you have everything selected (and matching the above screenshot), click the "OK" button to apply your settings and return to VirtualBox. From there, double-click on your "Test Bootloader" VM to start it. Once your VM starts up, you should see the words "Hello world!" printed on the screen.

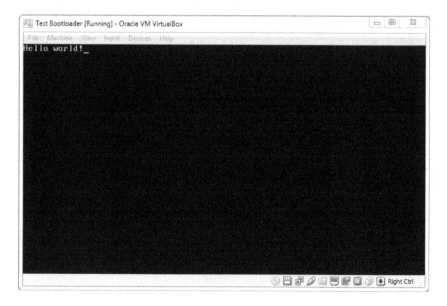

Creating the Entry Point

At the beginning of this chapter, we learned that once the bootloader has executed, its final job is to load the kernel into physical memory address 0x10000000 which will load the rest of the operating system. But, in order for our bootloader to know where the entry point into the kernel is, we will have to tell it by building out the actual kernel.

Even though the entire kernel can either be written completely in Assembly or completely in C, we will go with a mixed method here by separating the actual entry point from the rest of the kernel. For that, we will write the entry point in Assembly and leave the rest for the C programming language which we will drill into in the next chapter. The reason for separating the entry point from the rest of the kernel and including the entry point in this chapter as opposed to the next is so that we can expand on what we have learned so far about where each piece of our operating system gets loaded into memory. With that said, let's jump right into building the entry point of our kernel.

Just as we did in the previous section when creating the file for our bootloader, make sure you are in the CentOS development environment running in VirtualBox and click on **Applications > Accessories > gedit** to open the text editor we will be using for writing our code. Then, click on **File > New** (or press Ctrl + N or click the white-paper icon on the toolbar) to open a new / blank file. Type the following code into that new file and save the file as "**start.asm**". Whereas we created our bootloader in a folder on our Desktop called "bootloader", we will create the remaining files in a new folder on the Desktop called "**my_os**". This will be the location where we save all of our files, compile our operating system, and build the ISO which we will use later for testing our operating system. Since we will not be using the bootloader we created in the previous section, there is no need to have it in the same folder as the rest of our code. But, it is OK if you do choose to put them all in the same folder for easy reference.

start.asm

```
bits 32
global _start
```

```
extern main
section .text
_start:
 cli
 mov esp, stack
 call main
 hlt

section .bss
resb 8192
stack:
```

As mentioned before, the code above will act as the entry point into our operating system. It begins by notifying the NASM compiler that it should compile this code for 32-bit processors as indicated by the "**bits 32**" directive on the first line (as opposed to the "**bits 16**" directive in our bootloader code from before). Although this line isn't required − the compiler will figure it out on its own, it is still best practice to explicitly declare it here. This can make it easy to identify places that need to be changed later on when compiling the operating system to run on different architectures.

The second line ("**global _start**") should already look familiar. As mentioned in Chapter 3, this line tells the linker (which we will learn about in Chapter 8) where the program execution begins. From Chapter 3, you will recall that we placed this directive just after the "**section .text**" line and just before the "**_start:**" line. We could have done the same here, but I wanted to demonstrate that we can actually place the **global** directive in different locations since the linker will locate it regardless of its location.

The third line ("**extern main**") in the code above indicates that the "**main**" procedure can be found in an "**extern**al" file. As learned earlier in this book, the **main** function is the entry point into all applications. However, since we already have an entry point into our operating system (which we declared in our Assembly code using "**_start**"), we can actually rename the **main** function here to anything we want. But, to keep with what we have already learned in this book (and for following best practice), we will leave our procedure named "**main**". Whatever you name this, though, keep it in mind as we will see it again a few lines down in our entry code.

The next line ("**section .text**" - which we also learned about in Chapter 3) tells the compiler that the following lines will be the actual code that handles the processing. The first thing we do in this section (aka "function" or "procedure") is to disable (or **cl**ear) **i**nterrupts by using the "**cli**" command. This is done because other instructions such as the "**hlt**" (halt) instruction can awake the CPU, telling it to do other things – sometimes unintended.

After we have disabled interrupts, we then allocate some memory for the stack and point the stack pointer (**esp**) to it. The **stack** itself is defined as the last function in the file (indicated by "**stack:**"). As you will notice, there is a colon after **stack** which indicates it is a function. But, since there are no other instructions after it, this indicates that the function is currently empty. That is because we haven't added anything to the stack as of yet. We are just allocating memory for it and mapping it to the stack pointer.

The next line ("**call main**") is where we tell the system that it should now execute the instructions found in our "**main**" function. Again, this function will be provided by our kernel's C code which we will define in a separate file in the next chapter. Because the function is in a different file, we had to alert the compiler to this by using the "**extern**" instruction earlier. That is why I asked you to make note of whatever you chose to name this function. Plus, you will be using this same name in your **kernel.c** file in the next chapter. So, again, it is best to just stick with calling it "**main**" for now.

After we have told the system to call our **main** procedure, the only instruction we have left is to tell the system to "**halt**" as defined by the "**hlt**" instruction. The reason we want our system to halt for now is because we have nothing left for the CPU to process. Later on we will omit this instruction because we will want the CPU to continue processing further commands (such as user input). So, there will be no need for the system to halt at that time.

After the **.text** section, you will find the **.bss** section. As explained in Chapter 3, this section is where we define our variables. In this particular example, we use the "**resb**" instruction which reserves 8KB of memory for our stack. The "**res**" part of the instruction represents "**res**erve" while the "**b**" part of the instruction represents "**b**ytes". You could have just as easily used "**resw**" to reserve a "**w**ord", "**resd**" to reserve a "**d**ouble", or "**resq**" to reserve an array of ten reals. But, "**resb**" is all we need for our purposes.

GNU GRUB

That's it! We now have ourselves a nice shiny bootloader. However, since we want our operating system to boot on various devices using a specific kernel configuration, we will be using a bootloader from the GNU Project called "**GNU GRUB**" (short for "**GNU GR**and **U**nified **B**ootloader") instead of the bootloader we learned to build earlier in the chapter. Not only will this bootloader allow us to bootstrap the kernel, but it will also allow us to boot one of multiple operating systems should we decide later on to add multiple / different OSes.

In order for us to use GRUB, we will need to make a few additions to our kernel's entry code so that it follows the multiboot specification that GRUB requires. To do that, we will only need to add four additional lines to the beginning of our **.text** section which are indicated in bold below.

start.asm

```
bits 32
global _start
extern kernel_early
extern main

section .text
    align 4
    dd 0x1BADB002         ; magic
    dd 0x00               ; flags
    dd - (0x1BADB002 + 0x00) ; checksum
```

```
_start:
  cli
  mov esp, stack
  call kernel_early
  call main
  hlt

section .bss
resb 8192
stack:
```

The first of these additional lines ("**align 4**") is a directive that allows you to enforce alignment of the instruction or data immediately after the directive. Whatever number follows the **align** directive must be a power of 2 (i.e. 2, 4, 8, 16, 32, …) and must not be greater than the default alignment of the segment which we defined by saying that this should compile for a 32-bit system (i.e. "**bits 32**"). Since the system is expected to be 32 bits (i.e. 4 bytes), we must use alignment values that are less than or equal to 4.

The next line we added for the header ("**dd 0x1BADB002**") is a double-word (i.e. 4 bytes) that indicates a "magic" field that is required by GRUB. The next line ("**dd 0x00**") is where we define "flags" that are needed by GRUB. Since we will not be needing any additional flags at this time, we will simply set this field to zero. The third line ("**dd − (0x1BADB002 + 0x00)**") is a checksum that, when added to the values of the **magic** and **flags** fields, should always be equal to zero.

Aside from the additional header code, everything else in the code above will be the same as before except for one last thing. As you will see near the top of the code, I have added the line "*extern kernel_early*" as indicated by italics. Since it is an **extern** directive, you already know that the function will be located in an **extern**al file. Also, just before our **call main** line, you will see another line that calls the **kernel_early** function which we will define in our **kernel.c** file in the next chapter.

Although these lines aren't necessarily required for our operating system, I wanted to include them anyways as a way to demonstrate how we can name our functions differently as well as include multiple external calls. The reason for naming this procedure "**kernel_early**" and calling it before our call to "**main**" is so that we will have a way to execute instructions that need to be run prior to our kernel actually doing its thing. In this case, we will use the **kernel_early** function for initializing our terminal which we will use from within the kernel's **main** function. Other times we may also want to include other instructions in our Assembly file between the two **call** instructions for doing things such as re-enabling interrupts (using the "**sti**" instruction – short for "**st**art **i**nterrupts"), allocating more memory, or switching between real mode and protected mode as explained earlier.

Compiling the Entry Point

Now that we have our kernel's entry point, it is time to compile it. This is where we will use the NASM Assembly compiler we learned about in Chapter 5. To compile our entry point, click on **Assembly > Utilities > Terminal** which will open a prompt where the following commands need to be executed.

```
# cd ~/Desktop/my_os/
# nasm -f elf32 start.asm -o start.o
```

The first command above will change directories into the "**my_os**" folder we created on our Desktop that contains the source code for our operating system. The second line tells **nasm** to compile our Assembly code into machine code. The "**-f**" flag tells **nasm** what type of architecture it should compile the code for. Since we are building an operating system intended to be run on a 32-bit architecture, we will pass "**elf32**" as the architecture output format. The "**elf**" part stands for "**E**xecutable and **L**inkable **F**ormat" and the "**32**" part should be pretty evident at this point. With that said, you can also just pass "**elf**" as the output type and **nasm** will assume you meant "**elf32**".

For a list of other output formats we can compile Assembly code into using **nasm**, we can execute "**nasm -hf**" as described in the Appendix at the end of this book.

If everything worked correctly, you should be dropped back to the command prompt with nothing output to the screen. To verify that your Assembly file did compile correctly, run the "**ls**" command and you should see a file called "**start.o**".

⌐   ⌐   ⌐   ⌐   ⌐   ⌐   ⌐   ⌐   ⌐   ⌐   ⌐   ⌐   ⌐   ⌐   ⌐

At this point we now have a multi-boot loader that will boot our kernel which we will build in the next chapter. But before moving on, there is one last thing I would like to mention. Since different processors utilize different architectures, Assembly code can very much be architecture specific. That means, what works for one architecture might not / most likely does not work for another architecture. This is especially true when making system calls. Keep this in mind when developing operating systems for embedded devices, especially those devices built for the *Internet of Things*.

0x07 Welcome to the Kernel

If the operating system is the heart of a computer, you can think of the kernel as the brain. It is the central piece of the operating system that loads first, always remains in memory, and is responsible for managing low level hardware such as the storage device, memory, processor, and network card. Any time software further up in the stack wishes to communicate with low level hardware, it does so by sending requests to the kernel which in turn get passed on to the hardware. Basically, it is also the job of the kernel to make sure that every application that gets ran is allocated sufficient memory and CPU time.

When dealing with OS kernels, there are two types available. The first type is what is known as a "monolithic kernel". This type of kernel contains the majority of the operating system, including drivers to low level hardware as mentioned above. Since monolithic kernels contain most / all of the underlying operating system, these types of kernels are typically loaded into a protected area of memory so that other applications cannot tamper with them while in use. This protected - see privileged - area is known as the "kernel space". This space is separated from the space where applications are run, which is known as the "user space".

The second type of kernel is what is known as a "microkernel". This type of kernel is typically only responsible for two things: memory management and CPU management. All other functions get moved outside of the kernel which allows them to live and die (i.e. "crash") without bringing down the entire system (such as what happens when a device driver or other piece of software fails in a monolithic kernel). Where monolithic kernels run the entire operating system within the kernel space, microkernel systems only run the most critical activities in the kernel space and everything else is run in the user space.

Unlike monolithic kernels, microkernels are quite difficult to develop and debug. Operating systems such as Linux utilize monolithic kernels because they are easier to develop. Therefore, the kernel we will be building will be monolithic as well. By the way, do not get "monolithic" in this context confused with "non-modular". Monolithic kernels *do* support modularity such as the case of device drivers. In this case, modules are attached to the monolithic kernel which in turn increases the overall size of the kernel, yet it still remains monolithic since it (the kernel) and the modules are still run in the kernel space.

For an easy way of understanding how the kernel works, the kernel we will be building in this chapter will only have three functions: 1) initialize and clear the screen 2) print "Hello world" 3) return control to the bootloader which will halt the CPU. In Chapter 11, we will build on this functionality by extending our kernel to handle other things such as accepting user input via the keyboard.

Before we can start printing stuff to the screen, the first thing we need to do is declare a few variables. Since we will be referencing these variables from multiple functions, we will need to define them globally which we can do by adding them directly to the top of our code (i.e. outside of any functions – identified by curly braces { and }).

In order to print text to the screen like we want to do in our operating system, we will need to begin by gaining access to the physical memory that has been allocated for our video buffer. To do that, we will need to create a pointer to the address space which is always located at address **0xb8000** in protected mode for color monitors and **0xb0000** for monochrome monitors. Since this is a text buffer, our variable will need to be a pointer of type **char** like so:

static char* const VGA_MEMORY = (char*)0xb8000;

As you can see above, the allocated memory space for video in our operating system will begin at **0xb8000**. This buffer is capable of holding twenty five lines with each line consisting of eighty ascii characters. Therefore, the next two variables we will need to define will contain the width and height of our terminal.

static const int VGA_WIDTH = 80;
static const int VGA_HEIGHT = 25;

To understand how the video memory buffer is used, it is worth noting that the characters in our video buffer are represented by two bytes aligned as a 16-bit word. The lower byte is the actual character itself while the upper byte contains the format of the character such as its color, blinking, character set, and so on.

That's it for our global variable declarations. In Chapter 10 we will add more global variables when it comes time to start the architecture library for our operating system. But for now, these are all the variables we will need to define in order for our operating system to function. In fact, since we are only using these variables within one function at the moment, we could have just as easily placed them inside that single function. But, since later on we will be using these variables from multiple functions, it is wise to define them globally now.

As you will recall in the previous chapter, we added a line in our assembly code for **call kernel_early**. The idea there was to provide us with a place to do things (such as initializing and clearing the screen) that we want to happen before jumping into the functionality of the kernel itself. Even though we have already initialized our screen when we created a pointer to the video memory address space, we could have done other things inside of this function such as painting the background a different color or drawing a logo. Regardless, since we added that line to our Assembly code, we will now need to create that function here. For now, it will just be an empty function as follows:

```
void kernel_early(void) {
        // do something here
}
```

With that out of the way, the next thing we will need to do is define our **main** function which we learned in a previous chapter is the entry point into all applications. Since our "real" entry point was defined in our Assembly file (remember "**global _start**"?), we could have named our **main** function anything we wanted. But, for illustration purposes, we chose to stick with naming it "**main**" which is what we will also use in our kernel code like so:

```
int main(void *) {
        return 0;
}
```

As you can see, our **main** function has been defined as type "**int**" which means it is expected to return an **int**eger, hence the "**return 0;**" inside the function. Since the function isn't expecting any incoming parameters, the "**void**" statement between the parentheses indicates an empty argument list. The **void** could have been omitted, but I chose to include it here as best practice. Also, instead of setting the return type as **int** and returning **0** (zero) at the end, we could have also omitted the **return 0;** and substituted **int main(void *) {** with **void main(void *) {**. But, again, I went with this approach as it is best practice. Plus, using **void main(void *) {** instead of **int main(void *) {** doesn't work with some compilers. Also, the **return 0;** line indicates that the system terminated without any abnormalities. If the system terminates unexpectedly for any other reason, you can instead return a non-zero value where the value can be mapped to a list of error codes that describe what went wrong with the system.

Moving on. The first piece of code we will need to define at the top of our **main** function will be the string of text that we plan on printing to the screen – "**Hello world**" in this case. Since this variable will never change, we can define it as a **const**ant as shown below. This line (and all following lines) will need to be inserted inside the **main** function before the **return**.

const char *str = "Hello world";

In order for us to set each character in our video memory, we will need to define a new variable that will be the place holder for our current position within the video memory buffer. Likewise, we will also need to define a second variable that will act as the place holder for the current character position when iterating over the text string that we will be printing to the screen one character at a time.

unsigned int i = 0; // place holder for text string position
unsigned int j = 0; // place holder for video buffer position
As I just mentioned, we will be iterating through our text string and printing the string to the screen one character at a time. To iterate over that string, we will use a "**while**" loop that will run until it has discovered its first null byte. Even though we never explicitly defined a null byte in our text string, a null byte does exist at the very end since there is nothing left in the variable after our text. This can easily be seen if you were to examine the code when it has been loaded into memory and dumped to the console in hexadecimal values.

In the C programming language, null character values in ascii are indicated by '**\0**' (backslash zero). Knowing this, we can define our **while** loop like so:

```
while (str[i] != '\0') {
}
```

Inside of that **while** loop is where we will pass each character of our text string to the video buffer. Since we learned earlier that each character is expected to be passed as two bytes (one byte for the character and a second byte for the format of that character), we will need to add two updates to the video buffer. Since we are iterating through each character of our text string one character at a time, we will need to increment our **i** variable (place holder for our text string position) by one each time we pass through our **while** loop. We will also need to increment our **j** variable (place holder for our video buffer position) while we are at it. However, where our **i** variable gets incremented by *one* each time we iterate (because we want *one* character at a time), our **j** variable will be incremented by *two* each time we iterate (because we are setting values in our video buffer *two* bytes at a time).

```
VGA_MEMORY[j] = str[i];
VGA_MEMORY[j + 1] = 0x07;
i++;
j = j + 2;
```

As mentioned before, the upper byte of each character in the video memory buffer is a format flag. In the code above, you will see that we have used **"0x07"** which tells the system that this particular character should be formatted with a light grey color. If you would like to use a different color for your text (or you would like to use a different color for every character), here is a list of colors available to you.

VGA Color Codes

Black	0
Blue	1
Green	2
Cyan	3
Red	4
Magenta	5
Brown	6
Light Grey	7
Dark Grey	8
Light Blue	9
Light Green	10
Light Cyan	11
Light Red	12
Light Magenta	13
Light Brown	14
White	15

So that you don't have to attempt to create the entire kernel using the code snippets above, you can find the kernel code in its entirety below.

kernel.c

```
static char* const VGA_MEMORY = (char*)0xb8000;

static const int VGA_WIDTH = 80;
static const int VGA_HEIGHT = 25;

void kernel_early(void) {
        // do some early work here
```

```
}

int main(void) {
        const char *str = "Hello world";
        unsigned int i = 0; // place holder for text string position
        unsigned int j = 0; // place holder for video buffer position

        while (str[i] != '\0') {
                VGA_MEMORY[j] = str[i];
                VGA_MEMORY[j + 1] = 0x07;
                i++;
                j = j + 2;
        }
        return 0;
}
```

That's it. You now have yourself a working kernel. But, before we get too excited, we need to make sure it will compile successfully. To do that, open a terminal window and change directory to where your kernel.c file is located. If you are using the same naming conventions as I have been throughout this book, your kernel.c file should be located in a folder on your Desktop called "**my_os**". If so, you can use the following commands to get to that location and compile the kernel.

cd ~/Desktop/my_os/
gcc -c kernel.c -o kernel -ffreestanding -m32

The arguments for the **gcc** (**GNU C C**ompiler) are fairly self-explanatory. But, I will run through them real quick anyways. The **-c** flag tells the compiler that **kernel.c** is the input file that it will be compiling. The **-o** flag tells the compiler that the output / compiled file will be **kernel.o**. Unlike the first two flags, the **-ffreestanding** flag might be new to you. Basically, it tells the compiler that the standard C library may not exist and that the entry point may not necessarily be located at **main**. Remember, since we are building an entirely new operating system from scratch, we do not have the luxury of utilizing pre-existing C libraries like we do when developing other applications. Because of this, every function we utilize we will need to write ourselves. Otherwise, when we deploy our app / OS, the code we write may or may not work. The **-m32** flag simply tells the compiler that it should compile our code for a 32-bit architecture.

You now have yourself a new and shiny kernel. By combining your new kernel with the entry point you built in the last chapter, you are only a few steps away from having your very own operating system. In the next chapter, we will bring these pieces together to build that operating system and test it out for the very first time.

0x08 Putting it all Together

Before we can test our operating system, we will need to link the object files we created for the entry point and kernel. To do that, we will create a linker file that **gcc** will use to link those object files into a single executable kernel that we can boot with. Once we are finished with that, we will then create a **Makefile** that will take care of compiling the Assembly entry point and C kernel along with using our linker file to create that executable / bootable kernel. This file will also take care of building an **ISO** file which we will use to create the virtual machine (VM) where we can test our operating system and admire it in all its glory. Now, I know that all sounds like a lot of work, but it really isn't. So, we will just jump right in.

In your CentOS environment, open **gedit** as before. Then, create a new file and save it as "**linker.ld**" in the same folder that you created your **start.asm** and **kernel.c** files (i.e. in the "**my_os**" folder on your Desktop). At the top of that file, add the following line which will, just like in our Assembly code in Chapter 6, tell the system where the entry point (i.e. "**_start**") to our code can be found.

ENTRY (_start)

Below that, we will add a place to define the sections that we listed in our Assembly code (i.e. "**.text**" and "**.bss**"). If we had also included a "**.data**" section as mentioned in an earlier chapter, we would also declare that section here as well. At that point, **gcc** would merge the **.data** and **.bss** sections into one and place them after the "**.text**" section that contains all of our executable code. Remember, the **.bss** section is where we define changeable variables and the **.data** section is where we store global variables such as initialized data and constants.

```
SECTIONS
{
  . = 0x10000000;
  .text : { *(.text) }
  .bss : { *(.bss) }
}
```

In Chapter 6, we learned that the kernel is always loaded into physical address **0x10000000**. Well, as you can see in the code above, this is where we declare that address and tell the system where our executable code can be found once it is loaded into memory. The period (.) on the left side of the equals sign represents the location counter which is always initialized to **0x0**.

The asterisk (*) before each section name within the curly braces indicates a wildcard. This tells the compiler to locate any executable code (**.text**) from all input files (*), which we will define shortly, and merge it all into the .text section that we have defined here. The same is true for the .bss section as well. But, instead of executable code (.text), it tells the compiler to look for all global variables (**.bss**) from all input files (*) and to compile those into the .bss section we have defined here.

That's it. That is everything you need for your **linker.ld** file. Below is that file in its entirety to prove it.

linker.ld

```
ENTRY (_start)
SECTIONS
{
  . = 0x100000;
  .text : { *(.text) }
  .bss  : { *(.bss) }
}
```

Now that we have our linker file, the only thing we have left to do is to compile everything. But, instead of manually typing out every compile command into a terminal, we are going to ease our pains by building a reusable **Makefile**. Since you are already familiar with the commands for compiling the entry point and kernel, and because you can easily learn how **Makefile**s work with a quick Internet search, I am going to skip most of the details here and just show you the code.

In your CentOS development environment, open **gedit** once more and add the following code to a new file. Then, save that file as "**Makefile**" (with no file extension) into the same location as your **start.asm**, **kernel.c**, and **linker.ld** files. This file will be read by the "**make**" tool.

As per Wikipedia, "***make*** *is a utility that automatically builds executable programs and libraries from source code by reading files called Makefiles which specify how to derive the target program.*"

Makefile

```
CC=gcc
TARGET=myos
C_FILES=./kernel.c
OBJS=$(C_FILES:.c=.o)

all compile: $(TARGET)
all: finale
.PHONY: all compile clean finale

%.o:
        $(CC) -c $(@:.o=.c) -o $@ -ffreestanding -fno-exceptions -m32

$(TARGET): $(OBJS)
        $(shell nasm -f elf start.asm -o start.o)
        $(CC) -m32 -nostdlib -nodefaultlibs -lgcc start.o  $? -T linker.ld -o
$(TARGET)

finale:
        $(shell cd ~/Desktop/my_os/)
        $(shell cp $(TARGET) ./iso/boot/$(TARGET))
        $(shell grub2-mkrescue iso --output=$(TARGET).iso)

clean:
        rm -f *.o $(TARGET) $(TARGET).iso
        find . -name \*.o | xargs --no-run-if-empty rm
```

Before we can check that everything compiles correctly, there is one more thing we need to do to wrap up development. As explained in Chapter 6, we will be using a utility called "**GNU GRUB**" (short for "**GNU GR**and **U**nified **B**ootloader") that will allow us to compile our operating system for various systems using the specific kernel we built in the last chapter. But, before we can use the **GRUB** utility, we first need to create a configuration file that tells **GRUB** what to do.

Back in your CentOS development environment, open a command terminal and run the following command.

mkdir -p ~/Desktop/my_os/iso/boot/grub/

This will create a subfolder called "**iso**" in the same folder as your source code. Inside that folder, another folder called "**boot**" will be created which will include a subfolder within it called "**grub**". This folder structure is required by the **grub2-mkrescue** utility that we will learn about shortly.

Next, use **gedit** to create a new file and save it into the **~/Desktop/my_os/iso/boot/grub/** folder named "**grub.cfg**". This is the configuration file that will tell **grub** how it should create our **iso** which we will use in the next chapter. Since it is pretty much self-explanatory, here is the code that you will need to add into your **grub.cfg** file.

grub.cfg

```
set timeout=0
set default=0
menuentry "My Cool OS" {
        multiboot /boot/myos
}
```

As mentioned before, you should already be familiar with most of the commands listed in the **Makefile**. The one section I do want to point out, however, is the "**finale**". As you can see in the **Makefile** code above, this section makes a call out to the **shell** that tells it to change directory into the location where we created our operating system files (i.e.

"**~/Desktop/my_os/**" - assuming you followed the naming conventions in this book). Then, it makes another call out to the **shell** telling it to copy the compiled executable kernel into the "**/iso/boot/**" folder we just created. After that, it tells the **grub2-mkrescue** utility to generate an **iso** file that we will use in the next chapter for creating our VirtualBox VM and testing our operating system.

To verify that our **Makefile** works and that our operating system can compile successfully, click on **Applications > Utilities > Terminal** and run the following command:

make

If everything compiled successfully, you should now see some extra files in your OS folder: **start.o**, **kernel.o**, and **myos**. The main file to check for here is the "**myos**" file. This is the binary file for your executable kernel. If you want to also have your **Makefile** cleanup your OS folder a bit by removing the compiled object files (which is a good idea to do before re-running the **make** utility to prevent compilation using stale files), you can add the word "**clean**" to the end of the "**all: finale**" line inside your **Makefile**. Then, whenever you run the **make** utility from here on, it will call the "**clean**" section located at the bottom of the **Makefile** which will remove all compiled object files from your OS folder (i.e., all files that have the "**.o**" file extension) as well as your compiled kernel binary.

⅃　　⅃　　⅃　　⅃　　⅃　　⅃　　⅃　　⅃　　⅃　　⅃　　⅃　　⅃　　⅃　　⅃　　⅃

Congratulations! You now have a brand new operating system that you built yourself! And now is the time where you get to enjoy the fruits of your labor. In the next chapter, we will finally get to test our new shiny operating system (and show it off to all of our soon-to-be jealous friends)! So, let's get right to it.

0x09 Testing Your Operating System

So you've learned how the underlying mechanics of a computer work, got an introduction to the Assembly and C programming languages, and have gone through the [little] work of writing on your own operating system. Now comes the fun part! It is now time to test your shiny new operating system and admire it in all its glory. Thankfully, we already have some experience in doing this. Just like we did in Chapter 5 when we setup our CentOS development environment, we will go through the same process for creating a new virtual machine using VirtualBox.

Before we can create a new VM (Virtual Machine) for testing our new operating system, we will need to copy the ISO that we created in the last chapter over to our Windows host computer. Luckily for us, we have already taken the necessary steps to make this an easy task (Remember in Chapter 5 when we installed the VirtualBox Guest Additions?).

To copy your compiled ISO from your VirtualBox guest machine over to your Windows host machine, begin by launching Windows Explorer on your Windows host machine and navigate to a location where you would like to copy your ISO to. For now, you can choose your Desktop if you'd like. Just make sure you select a place that you will easily remember in the next step.

Over in your VirtualBox CentOS guest environment, click on **Places > Home** and navigate to **~/Desktop/my_os/** (or where ever you saved your source code and created your ISO). Next, right-click on the ISO ("**myos.iso**") in your CentOS environment and select "**Copy**". Then, right-click on your Windows Explorer in your Windows environment and select "**Paste**".

Note: If you have any issues copying and pasting from your CentOS guest machine to your Windows machine, you can resize your VirtualBox window so that you can position it on top of Window Explorer where you can drag the ISO from CentOS to Windows Explorer. Also, if you do not want to copy from CentOS to Windows, you can always install VirtualBox in your CentOS environment and create a VM within that VM.

Now that you have your ISO copied to your Windows host machine, it is time to create the VM. To do that, begin by opening the Oracle VM VirtualBox Manager and clicking the blue "**New**" button on the toolbar or by going to **Machine > New**. This will open a modal window that will ask you about the virtual machine you are attempting to create.

For the "**Name**" field, type in something cool such as "**My Cool OS**" or "**My Bad Ass OS**". Next, select "**Other**" for the "**Type**" field and "**Other/Unknown**" for the "**Version**" field. Since our operating system doesn't do much [yet], we can set the "**Memory size**" to something like "**8 MB**" or less. Since we also do not have anything in our OS for accessing a file system, there is no need for selecting a hard disk. So, under "**Hard disk**", select the first option for "**Do not add a virtual hard disk**". After that, click the "**Create**" button.

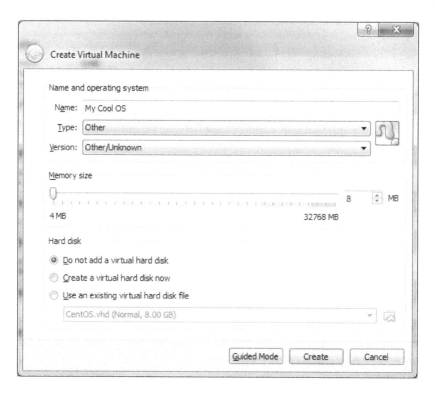

Back in the Oracle VM VirtualBox Manager, you should now see your new operating system ("**My Cool OS**") listed on the left below your "**CentOS**" VM. You can now launch that VM by either double-clicking the VM in the list or by single-clicking it and then clicking the green "**Start**" button on the toolbar. Just like when we were creating our CentOS VM, VirtualBox will now display a dialog window asking us to "**Select start-up disk**". Click the folder-arrow icon at the right of the drop-down, navigate to your Desktop (or where ever you copied your ISO), and select your ISO.

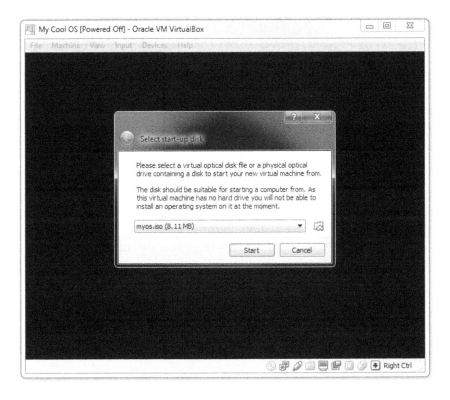

The only thing you have left to do now is click the "**Start**" button. It will only take a second and voila! You should now see "**Hello world**" printed inside a black window. This is your operating system. Congratulations! Give yourself a pat on the back!

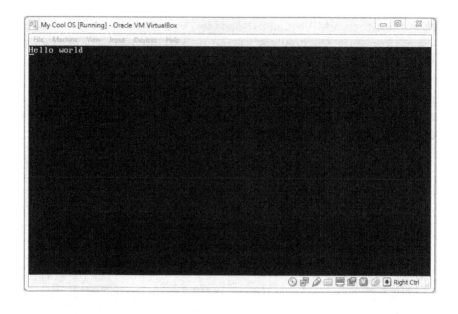

I know it doesn't look like much right now, but this is the beginning of many great things that you can do from here on. And, to help you get started with making your new operating system do those great things, the next couple of chapters will walk you through starting your architecture library and expanding your OS to do even more.

0x0A Starting Your Architecture Library

So we have ourselves a brand new operating system. Now what? Well, now we will begin to grow that operating system into something bigger and better by providing it with more capabilities. We will do that by starting a library that can be used with different system architectures. Since we have already designed our operating system for the x86 architecture, we will continue with that by expanding our console capabilities.

Again, you have to remember that since we are building a completely new operating system from scratch, we do not have the C libraries that other operating systems provide. Therefore, we are solely responsible for building out all of the additional functionality for even the simplest of functions from here on.

Before we can start adding to what our console is capable of, we first need to add in several utility methods. Although not all of these utilities will be used in the architecture code we will look at in this chapter, it is still a nice idea to list them now as they will be used extensively in other parts of our operating system and other applications.

To get started, open the file explorer in your CentOS development environment and navigate to where you have created your operating system. Inside that folder, create two subfolders called "**kernel**" and "**libc**". The **kernel** folder is where we will be adding our architecture specific code and the **libc** folder is where we will create the following utilities. For now, navigate into the **libc** folder and create two subfolders called "**include**" and "**string**". Within the **include** folder, create a file called "**string.h**" with the following code:

string.h

```
#ifndef _STRING_H
#define _STRING_H 1

#include "stddef.h"
```

```
int memcmp(const void* aptr, const void* bptr, size_t size);size_t
strlen(const char*);
char* strcat(char* d, const char* s);
char* strcpy(char* d, const char* s);
int strcmp(const char * s1, const char * s2);
char *strncat(char *dest, const char *src, size_t n);
char *strncpy(char *dest, const char *src, size_t n);
char *strstr(char *s1, const char *s2);
char *strchr(const char *s, int c);
int strncmp(const char * s1, const char * s2, size_t n);
```

```
#endif
```

This code simply lists out the available functions that we will define in the next utilities.

Next, inside the **string** folder, create individual files using the following file names and code.

ctos.c

```
#include "../include/string.h"

char *ctos(char s[2], const char c)
{
    s[0] = c;
    s[1] = '\0';
    return s;
}
```

This utility converts a single character into a NULL terminated string.

memcmp.c

```
#include "../include/string.h"

int memcmp(const void* aptr, const void* bptr, size_t size)
{
```

```
        const unsigned char* a = (const unsigned char*) aptr;
        const unsigned char* b = (const unsigned char*) bptr;
        size_t i;
        for ( i = 0; i < size; i++ )
                if ( a[i] < b[i] )
                        return -1;
                else if ( b[i] < a[i] )
                        return 1;
        return 0;
}
```

This utility accepts two memory areas and compares the first *n* bytes of the two.

memset.c

```
#include "../include/string.h"

void* memset(void* bufptr, int value, size_t size)
{
        unsigned char* buf = (unsigned char*) bufptr;
        size_t i;
        for ( i = 0; i < size; i++ )
                buf[i] = (unsigned char) value;
        return bufptr;
}
```

This utility fills the first *size* bytes of memory pointed to by *bufptr* with the constant byte *value*.

strlen.c

```
#include "../include/string.h"

size_t strlen(const char* str)
{
        size_t ret = 0;
        while ( str[ret] != 0 )
```

```
            ret++;
        return ret;
}
```

This utility accepts a character array and returns the length (i.e. number of characters) of that string.

strcpy.c

```
#include "../include/string.h"

char* strcpy(char* dest, const char* src) {
    char* tmp = dest;

    while ((*dest++ = *src++) != 0) ;

    return tmp;
}
```

This utility accepts two string arrays and copies the second string ("**src**") into the first string ("**dest**").

strcmp.c

```
#include "../include/string.h"

int strcmp(const char* s1, const char* s2)
{
    while(*s1 && (*s1 == *s2))
        s1++, s2++;
    return *(const unsigned char*)s1 - *(const unsigned char*)s2;
}
```

This utility accepts two string arrays and compares them. If the return value is less than zero, it indicates that **s1** is less than **s2**. If the return value is greater than zero, it indicates **s2** is less than **s1**. If the return value is equal to zero, it indicates that the two string arrays are the same.

strncmp.c

```
#include "../include/string.h"
#include "stddef.h"

int strncmp(const char* s1, const char* s2, size_t n)
{
    while(n--)
        if (*s1++ != *s2++)
            return *(unsigned char*)(s1 - 1) - *(unsigned char*)(s2 - 1);
    return 0;
}
```

Similar to the **strcmp** utility, this utility compares two string arrays as well. However, this utility accepts a third parameter that tells the utility to compare the first **n** characters of each string.

strchr.c

```
#include "../include/string.h"

char *strchr(const char *s, int c)
{
    while (*s != (char)c)
        if (!*s++)
            return 0;
    return (char *)s;
}
```

This utility accepts a string array and a character (represented as an **int**) and searches the string array for the existence of the character. If the character is found within the string array, a pointer to that character's location will be returned. Otherwise, it will return NULL.

strstr.c

```
#include "../include/string.h"

char *strstr(char *s1, const char *s2)
```

```
{
  size_t n = strlen(s2);
  while (*s1)
    if (!memcmp(s1++, s2, n))
      return s1 - 1;
  return 0;
}
```

Similar to the previous utility, this utility searches **s1** for the presence of **s2**. If the string array **s2** (i.e. the "needle") is found in the string array **s1** (i.e. the "haystack"), the utility will return a pointer to the location of **s2**. Otherwise, it will return zero.

strcat.c

```
#include "../include/string.h"

char* strcat(char* dest, const char* src) {
  char* tmp = dest;

  while (*dest) dest++;
  while ((*dest++ = *src++) != 0) ;

  return tmp;
}
```

This utility takes the string array **src** and appends it to the end of the **dest** string array and returns that concatenated value.

strutil.c

```
#include "../include/string.h"

int isupper(char c)
{
  return (c >= 'A' && c <= 'Z');
}
```

```c
int islower(char c)
{
    return (c >= 'a' && c <= 'z');
}

int isalpha(char c)
{
    return ((c >= 'A' && c <= 'Z') || (c >= 'a' && c <= 'z'));
}

int isspace(char c)
{
    return (c == ' ' || c == '\t' || c == '\n' || c == '\12');
}

int isdigit(char c)
{
    return (c >= '0' && c <= '9');
}

char *ltrim(char *s)
{
    while (isspace(*s)) s++;
    return s;
}

char *rtrim(char *s)
{
    char* back = s + strlen(s);
    while (isspace(*--back));
    *(back + 1) = '\0';
    return s;
}

char *trim(char *s)
{
```

```
    return rtrim(ltrim(s));
}
```

These utilities are fairly self-explanatory, especially to those that are familiar with programming. The first two utilities check if the incoming characters are uppercase or lowercase respectively. The third utility checks if the incoming character is a letter (i.e. A-Z). The fourth utility checks if the incoming character is a space. The fifth utility checks if the incoming character is a number (i.e. 0-9). The sixth utility will trim whitespaces from the left side of a string. The seventh utility will trim whitespaces from the right side of a string. And, the eighth utility will trim whitespaces from both the left and right sides of a string.

Expanding the Console

As mentioned before, most of the work we do in our kernel will be specific to the system architecture we are planning to run our operating system on. Because of that, we will need to create files that are also architecture specific. Since earlier I mentioned that we will be expanding our operating system by expanding the capabilities of our console, that is what the next couple of files will focus on.

Earlier inside our "**my_os**" folder, we created two subfolders called "**kernel**" and "**libc**". Inside the "**kernel**" folder, create a new file called "**tty.h**". This file is where we will list the different VGA colors as mentioned in Chapter 7. This is also where we will define the methods for "**printf**" that we will use to print strings to the console, "**terminal_initialize**" which we will use for setting up our console, and procedures for getting the current X and Y values of the cursor.

tty.h

```
#ifndef _TTY_H
#define _TTY_H 1

enum vga_color {
        COLOR_BLACK = 0,
```

```
        COLOR_BLUE = 1,
        COLOR_GREEN = 2,
        COLOR_CYAN = 3,
        COLOR_RED = 4,
        COLOR_MAGENTA = 5,
        COLOR_BROWN = 6,
        COLOR_LIGHT_GREY = 7,
        COLOR_DARK_GREY = 8,
        COLOR_LIGHT_BLUE = 9,
        COLOR_LIGHT_GREEN = 10,
        COLOR_LIGHT_CYAN = 11,
        COLOR_LIGHT_RED = 12,
        COLOR_LIGHT_MAGENTA = 13,
        COLOR_LIGHT_BROWN = 14,
        COLOR_WHITE = 15,
};

void terminal_initialize(void);
int printf(const char* format, ...);

int get_terminal_row(void);
int get_terminal_col(void);

#endif
```

Now that we have defined the procedures we will be calling from inside our kernel, it is now time for us to add the code that actually does the work. For that, create a new file called "**tty.c**" and save it within the same "**kernel**" folder where you created the "**tty.h**" file. Since you should already have a good understanding of how C code works, I won't bore you with the details of what is going on in this file. Instead, I will just show you the code as it is relatively straight forward and extremely simple to follow.

tty.c

```
#include "stdint.h"
#include "stddef.h"
```

```
#include "stdarg.h"
#include "tty.h"
#include "../libc/include/string.h"

static const size_t VGA_WIDTH = 80;
static const size_t VGA_HEIGHT = 25;

static uint16_t* const VGA_MEMORY = (uint16_t*) 0xb8000;

size_t terminal_row;
size_t terminal_column;
uint8_t terminal_color;
uint16_t* terminal_buffer;

static inline uint8_t make_color(enum vga_color fg, enum vga_color bg) {
        return fg | bg << 4;
}

static inline uint16_t make_vgaentry(char c, uint8_t color) {
        uint16_t c16 = c;
        uint16_t color16 = color;
        return c16 | color16 << 8;
}

void terminal_initialize(void) {
        terminal_row = 0;
        terminal_column = 0;
        terminal_color = make_color(COLOR_LIGHT_GREY, COLOR_BLACK);
        terminal_buffer = VGA_MEMORY;
        size_t y;
        for ( y = 0; y < VGA_HEIGHT; y++ ) {
                size_t x;
                for ( x = 0; x < VGA_WIDTH; x++ ) {
                        const size_t index = y * VGA_WIDTH + x;
                        terminal_buffer[index] = make_vgaentry(' ',
terminal_color);
```

```
                }
            }
}

void terminal_scroll()
{
   int i;
   for (i = 0; i < VGA_HEIGHT; i++){
         int m;
      for (m = 0; m < VGA_WIDTH; m++){
         terminal_buffer[i * VGA_WIDTH + m] = terminal_buffer[(i + 1) *
VGA_WIDTH + m];
      }
         terminal_row--;
   }
   terminal_row = VGA_HEIGHT - 1;
}

void terminal_putentryat(char c, uint8_t color, size_t x, size_t y) {
         const size_t index = y * VGA_WIDTH + x;
         terminal_buffer[index] = make_vgaentry(c, color);
}

void terminal_putchar(char c) {
         if (c == '\n' || c == '\r') {
                  terminal_column = 0;
                  terminal_row++;
                  if (terminal_row == VGA_HEIGHT)
                           terminal_scroll();
                  return;
         } else if (c == '\t') {
                  terminal_column += 4;
                  return;
         } else if (c == '\b') {
                  terminal_putentryat(' ', terminal_color, terminal_column--,
terminal_row);
```

```
                terminal_putentryat(' ', terminal_color, terminal_column,
terminal_row);
                return;
        }

        terminal_putentryat(c, terminal_color, terminal_column,
terminal_row);
        if ( ++terminal_column == VGA_WIDTH ) {
                terminal_column = 0;
                if ( ++terminal_row == VGA_HEIGHT ) {
                        terminal_row = 0;
                }
        }
}

void terminal_write(const char* data, size_t size) {
        size_t i;
        for ( i = 0; i < size; i++ )
                terminal_putchar(data[i]);
}

int putchar(int ic) {
        char c = (char)ic;
        terminal_write(&c, sizeof(c));
        return ic;
}

static void print(const char* data, size_t data_length) {
        size_t i;
        for ( i = 0; i < data_length; i++ )
                putchar((int) ((const unsigned char*) data)[i]);
}

int printf(const char* format, ...) {
        va_list parameters;
        va_start(parameters, format);
```

```
int written = 0;
size_t amount;
int rejected_bad_specifier = 0;

while ( *format != '\0' ) {
        if ( *format != '%' ) {
            print_c:
                amount = 1;
                while ( format[amount] && format[amount] != '%' )
                        amount++;
                print(format, amount);
                format += amount;
                written += amount;
                continue;
        }

        const char* format_begun_at = format;

        if ( *(++format) == '%' )
                goto print_c;

        if ( rejected_bad_specifier ) {
            incomprehensible_conversion:
                rejected_bad_specifier = 1;
                format = format_begun_at;
                goto print_c;
        }

        if ( *format == 'c' ) {
                format++;
                char c = (char) va_arg(parameters, int /* char
promotes to int */);
                print(&c, sizeof(c));
        } else if ( *format == 's' ) {
                format++;
                const char* s = va_arg(parameters, const char*);
```

```
                              print(s, strlen(s));
                    } else {
                              goto incomprehensible_conversion;
                    }
          }

          va_end(parameters);

          return written;
}

int get_terminal_row(void)
{
          return terminal_row;
}

int get_terminal_col(void)
{
          return terminal_column;
}
```

Now that we have those procedures out of the way, we need to reference the files we just created and make calls to the necessary procedures from inside our kernel. To do that, open up "**kernel.c**" and make the following changes.

kernel.c

```
#include "kernel/tty.h"

void kernel_early(void) {
          terminal_initialize();
}

__attribute__((noreturn))
int main(void) {
          printf("Hello world\n");
```

```
        while (1) { }
        return 0;
}
```

As you can see in the above code, the first line is where we reference the file that includes the definitions for "**printf**" and "**terminal_initialize**". Since those are the only two procedures we call from our kernel, those are the only two procedures we needed to define in our "**tty.h**" file. Next, inside the **kernel_early** function, we make a call to "**terminal_initialize**" which sets up our video memory and buffer. Then, inside our "**main**" function, we utilize the "**printf**" procedure we created before.

Before we can compile all of the code that we just added, we need to update our **Makefile** so that it too is aware of our new files. To do that, simply add the file names for each of the **.c** files to the **C_FILES** variable in your **Makefile**. When finished, it should look like the following where the items in bold are the changes made since we built this file in Chapter 8.

Makefile

```
CC=gcc
TARGET=myos
C_FILES=./libc/string/ctos.c \
        ./libc/string/memcmp.c \
        ./libc/string/memset.c \
        ./libc/string/strcat.c \
        ./libc/string/strchr.c \
        ./libc/string/strcmp.c \
        ./libc/string/strcpy.c \
        ./libc/string/strlen.c \
        ./libc/string/strncmp.c \
        ./libc/string/strstr.c \
        ./libc/string/strutil.c \
        ./kernel/tty.c \
        ./kernel.c
OBJS=$(C_FILES:.c=.o)
all compile: $(TARGET)
```

```
all: finale
.PHONY: all compile clean finale

%.o:
        $(CC) -c $(@:.o=.c) -o $@ -ffreestanding -fno-exceptions -m32

$(TARGET): $(OBJS)
        $(shell nasm -f elf start.asm -o start.o)
        $(CC) -m32 -nostdlib -nodefaultlibs -lgcc start.o $? -T linker.ld -o
$(TARGET)

finale:
        $(shell cd ~/Desktop/my_os/)
        $(shell cp $(TARGET) ./iso/boot/$(TARGET))
        $(shell grub2-mkrescue iso --output=$(TARGET).iso)

clean:
        rm -f *.o $(TARGET) $(TARGET).iso
        find . -name \*.o | xargs --no-run-if-empty rm
```

The only thing you have left to do now is compile everything by executing the "**make**" command again from your terminal. Once you have done that, follow the steps from Chapter 9 again to deploy and test your operating system to make sure you didn't miss anything.

0x0B Expanding Your OS

Now that we have started building out a working architecture-specific operating system, let's build on what we have done so far to expand our operating system even further. Even though I will be throwing a lot of code at you in this chapter, do not get discouraged. All of the code mentioned in this chapter can be downloaded in its entirety from my website at the link below. In fact, the source code for the entire operating system mentioned in this book is available in the ZIP file at the following address: http://www.lucuslabs.com/downloads/my_cool_os.zip

Note: This chapter contains more source code and less text. So, if you are happy with your current operating system, want to simply download the source code from my website, or want to move on to learning how to cross-compile for other architectures, please feel free to skip this chapter and return to it at a later time.

The first thing we will take a look at adding to our existing operating system is the ability to accept user input via the keyboard. In order to do that, we will make use of inline Assembly code which we haven't done yet, but is relatively straight forward. Doing this from C code is just as easy as doing it directly in Assembly. All you have to do is take the code you would normally write in Assembly and wrap it in parenthesis prefixed with "**asm**" or "**__asm__**" as in the case below.

You will also notice that we have also added the keyword "**__volatile__**" to the beginning of our Assembly code as well. The reason for doing this is because calling Assembly code from inside of C can sometimes produce unintentional side effects. This is in part due to the **gcc** (and similar) compilers that attempt to optimize the code during compilation. By prefixing Assembly code with "**__volatile__**" qualifier, it will tell the compiler to disable certain optimizations and basically execute the code "as-is".

As always, we will begin adding new functionality to our operating system by first defining the procedures that we are adding. For keyboard input, create a new file in your "**kernel**" folder (since this is architecture specific) called "**io.h**" and add the following code.

io.h

```
#ifndef _IO_H
#define _IO_H 1

#include "stdint.h"

/* The I/O ports */
#define FB_COMMAND_PORT     0x3d4
#define FB_DATA_PORT        0x3d5

/* The I/O port commands */
#define FB_HIGH_BYTE_COMMAND   0x0e
#define FB_LOW_BYTE_COMMAND    0x0f

uint8_t inb(uint16_t port);
void outb(uint16_t port, uint8_t val);
uint8_t scan(void);

void move_cursor(int row, int col);
void printprompt(void);

#endif
```

Next, create another file in the same location and name it "**io.c**" that contains the following code. Basically, all this code does is it takes a 8/16/32-bit value and either receives it in ("**inb**") from an I/O location or sends it out ("**outb**") to an I/O location. It also monitors the I/O port **0x60** (which is the keyboard port) for any input and returns incoming value values via the "**scan**" procedure. After that, there are procedures for moving the cursor on the screen and drawing a command prompt similar to the one found in Linux terminals (i.e., "**$>**").

io.c

```c
#include "io.h"
#include "tty.h"

uint8_t inb(uint16_t port)
{
    uint8_t ret;
    __asm__ __volatile__("inb %1, %0" : "=a" (ret) : "Nd" (port));
    return ret;
}

void outb(uint16_t port, uint8_t val)
{
    __asm__ __volatile__("outb %0, %1" : : "a" (val), "Nd" (port));
}

uint8_t scan(void)
{
    unsigned char brk;
    static uint8_t key = 0;
    uint8_t scan = inb(0x60);
    brk = scan & 0x80;
    scan = scan & 0x7f;
    if (brk)
            return key = 0;
    else if (scan != key)
            return key = scan;
    else
            return 0;
}

void move_cursor(int row, int col)
{
    unsigned short pos = (row * 80) + col;
    outb(FB_COMMAND_PORT, FB_LOW_BYTE_COMMAND);
    outb(FB_DATA_PORT, (unsigned char)(pos & 0xFF));
    outb(FB_COMMAND_PORT, FB_HIGH_BYTE_COMMAND);
```

```
    outb(FB_DATA_PORT, (unsigned char)((pos >> 8) & 0xFF));
}
void printprompt(void)
{
    printf("\n$> ");
    move_cursor(get_terminal_row(), get_terminal_col());
}
```

As we read data from I/O ports directly, the data that we get needs to be translated into something meaningful, at least from the user's standpoint. In the case of reading keyboard data, we will need to map the input to keys that are actually on the keyboard. To do that, we will create another file in our "**kernel**" folder called "**kbd.h**" which will hold the keyboard map for us. This file will also include a few other definitions (aka. "variables") that will make keyboard mapping easier.

kbd.h

```
#define KBSTATP      0x64   // kbd controller status port(I)
#define KBS_DIB      0x01   // kbd data in buffer
#define KBDATAP      0x60   // kbd data port(I)

#define NO           0

#define SHIFT        (1<<0)
#define CTL          (1<<1)
#define ALT          (1<<2)

#define CAPSLOCK     (1<<3)
#define NUMLOCK      (1<<4)
#define SCROLLLOCK   (1<<5)

#define EOESC        (1<<6)

// Special keycodes
#define KEY_HOME     0xE0
#define KEY_END      0xE1
```

```
#define KEY_UP          0xE2
#define KEY_DN          0xE3
#define KEY_LF          0xE4
#define KEY_RT          0xE5
#define KEY_PGUP        0xE6
#define KEY_PGDN        0xE7
#define KEY_INS         0xE8
#define KEY_DEL         0xE9

// C('A') == Control-A
#define C(x) (x - '@')

static char shiftcode[256] =
{
  [0x1D] CTL,
  [0x2A] SHIFT,
  [0x36] SHIFT,
  [0x38] ALT,
  [0x9D] CTL,
  [0xB8] ALT
};

static char togglecode[256] =
{
  [0x3A] CAPSLOCK,
  [0x45] NUMLOCK,
  [0x46] SCROLLLOCK
};

static char normalmap[256] =
{
  NO,  0x1B, '1', '2', '3', '4', '5', '6', // 0x00
  '7', '8', '9', '0', '-', '=', '\b', '\t',
  'q', 'w', 'e', 'r', 't', 'y', 'u', 'i', // 0x10
  'o', 'p', '[', ']', '\n', NO,  'a', 's',
  'd', 'f', 'g', 'h', 'j', 'k', 'l', ';', // 0x20
```

```
'\", '`', NO,  '\\', 'z', 'x', 'c', 'v',
'b', 'n', 'm', ',', '.', '/', NO,  '*', // 0x30
NO,  ' ', NO, NO, NO, NO, NO, NO,
NO, NO, NO, NO, NO, NO, NO, '7', // 0x40
'8', '9', '-', '4', '5', '6', '+', '1',
'2', '3', '0', '.', NO,  NO,  NO,  NO,  // 0x50
[0x9C] '\n',    // KP_Enter
[0xB5] '/',     // KP_Div
[0xC8] KEY_UP,   [0xD0] KEY_DN,
[0xC9] KEY_PGUP, [0xD1] KEY_PGDN,
[0xCB] KEY_LF,   [0xCD] KEY_RT,
[0x97] KEY_HOME, [0xCF] KEY_END,
[0xD2] KEY_INS,  [0xD3] KEY_DEL
};

static char shiftmap[256] =
{
NO,  033, '!', '@', '#', '$', '%', '^', // 0x00
'&', '*', '(', ')', '_', '+', '\b', '\t',
'Q', 'W', 'E', 'R', 'T', 'Y', 'U', 'I', // 0x10
'O', 'P', '{', '}', '\n', NO, 'A', 'S',
'D', 'F', 'G', 'H', 'J', 'K', 'L', ':', // 0x20
'"', '~', NO, '|', 'Z', 'X', 'C', 'V',
'B', 'N', 'M', '<', '>', '?', NO,  '*', // 0x30
NO,  ' ', NO, NO, NO, NO, NO, NO,
NO, NO, NO, NO, NO, NO, NO, '7', // 0x40
'8', '9', '-', '4', '5', '6', '+', '1',
'2', '3', '0', '.', NO,  NO,  NO,  NO,  // 0x50
[0x9C] '\n',    // KP_Enter
[0xB5] '/',     // KP_Div
[0xC8] KEY_UP,   [0xD0] KEY_DN,
[0xC9] KEY_PGUP, [0xD1] KEY_PGDN,
[0xCB] KEY_LF,   [0xCD] KEY_RT,
[0x97] KEY_HOME, [0xCF] KEY_END,
[0xD2] KEY_INS,  [0xD3] KEY_DEL
};
```

```
static char ctlmap[256] =
{
  NO,    NO,    NO,    NO,    NO,    NO,    NO,    NO,
  NO,    NO,    NO,    NO,    NO,    NO,    NO,    NO,
  C('Q'), C('W'), C('E'), C('R'), C('T'), C('Y'), C('U'), C('I'),
  C('O'), C('P'), NO,    NO,    '\r',  NO,    C('A'), C('S'),
  C('D'), C('F'), C('G'), C('H'), C('J'), C('K'), C('L'), NO,
  NO,    NO,    NO,    C('\\'), C('Z'), C('X'), C('C'), C('V'),
  C('B'), C('N'), C('M'), NO,    NO,    C('/'), NO,    NO,
  [0x9C] '\r',   // KP_Enter
  [0xB5] C('/'),  // KP_Div
  [0xC8] KEY_UP,  [0xD0] KEY_DN,
  [0xC9] KEY_PGUP, [0xD1] KEY_PGDN,
  [0xCB] KEY_LF,  [0xCD] KEY_RT,
  [0x97] KEY_HOME, [0xCF] KEY_END,
  [0xD2] KEY_INS, [0xD3] KEY_DEL
};
```

Before we can use the code from this chapter, we first need to compile it. That means we will need to update our **Makefile** to include the files we just finished creating. To do that, open up your **Makefile** and add the following files under your **C_FILES** variable.

./kernel/tty.c \
./kernel/io.c \

Your overall **C_FILES** variable should now look like this:

C_FILES

```
C_FILES=./libc/string/memcmp.c \
        ./libc/string/memset.c \
        ./libc/string/strcat.c \
        ./libc/string/strchr.c \
        ./libc/string/strcmp.c \
        ./libc/string/strcpy.c \
```

```
./libc/string/strlen.c \
./libc/string/strncmp.c \
./libc/string/strstr.c \
./libc/string/strutil.c \
./libc/string/ctos.c \
./kernel/tty.c \
./kernel/io.c \
./kernel.c
```

At this point we now have everything we need to accept user input via the keyboard and display that input in the console. So, all we have left to do now is update our **kernel.c** file to account for this user input and send it to the screen. While we are at it, we will also add some code to check incoming text for the presence of specific keyboards and will treat those accordingly. As you can see in the code below, I am checking for the presence of the single word "**exit**" and am printing the text "**Goodbye!**" to the screen if the user types the word "**exit**" and presses the enter key. You will also see that I continuously move the cursor to the new location after every keystroke and print a new line with the prompt ("**$>**") that we defined in our **io.c** file.

kernel.c

```
#include "kernel/tty.h"
#include "kernel/io.h"
#include "kernel/kbd.h"
#include "libc/include/string.h"

void kernel_early(void) {
        terminal_initialize();
}

int main(void) {
        char *buff;
        strcpy(&buff[strlen(buff)], "");
        printprompt();
        while (1) {
```

```
                uint8_t byte;
                while (byte = scan()) {
                        if (byte == 0x1c) {
                                if (strlen(buff) > 0 && strcmp(buff, "exit")
== 0)
                                        printf("\nGoodbye!");
                                printprompt();
                                memset(&buff[0], 0, sizeof(buff));
                                break;
                        } else {
                                char c = normalmap[byte];
                                char *s;
                                s = ctos(s, c);
                                printf("%s", s);
                                strcpy(&buff[strlen(buff)], s);
                        }
                        move_cursor(get_terminal_row(),
get_terminal_col());
                }
        }
        return 0;
}
```

That's it. We should now be able to compile our operating system using the **"make"** command that we learned about earlier, copy the newly created ISO to our Windows host machine, and create a new VM (Virtual Machine) just as we did in Chapter 9. If everything went accordingly, we should see something like the following whenever we test our updated operating system.

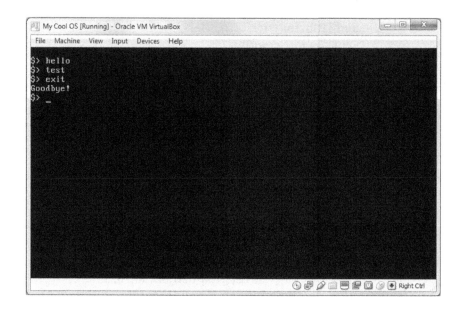

I will now leave it with you to expand your operating system to do all of the magical things you want it to do. However, I won't leave it with you blindly. Instead, I will leave you with a quick note to point you in the right direction should you have the need to add networking capabilities to your operating system (which I am sure you will).

When it comes time to add networking to your operating system, whether it is for desktop type systems or embedded systems, there are two TCP/IP stacks that I suggest you look into.

The first is called "**lwIP**" (**Light Weight IP**) which you can find at http://savannah.nongnu.org/projects/lwip/.

This is the networking library that I use the most when developing custom operating systems. It is one of the faster libraries (especially when compared to the next library I will mention) and includes DHCP as well as full UDP with multicast which are typically nice to have if not required, especially with embedded systems.

The second is called "**uIP**" which you can find at
https://github.com/adamdunkels/uip.

One of the best things about **uIP** is its small footprint. However, **uIP** uses polling which can constrain high throughput use cases and doesn't include DHCP out-of-the-box. If you need higher throughput than what **uIP** offers out-of-the-box, you can do some substantial tweaking to make it perform better.

If you have a little extra RAM and CPU, I would recommend going with **lwIP**. But, if resource limitations are a big factor in your project, you should take a look at **uIP**. I have used both libraries and both are capable of getting the job done. It just depends on what your use case is and how much additional coding and tweaking you don't mind doing.

0x0C Cross-Compiling for Other Architectures

Everything we have learned in this book so far has been about developing an operating system that works on the x86 architecture. However, since not all devices utilize an x86 processor (like many of those found in the *Internet of Things*), it is advantageous for us to also know how to develop and compile operating systems for other architectures as well. So, that is what we will address in this chapter.

Not only will we learn how to cross-compile our operating system for other architectures, but we will also learn how to build our own cross-compilers that will allow us to compile for even more architectures as well - the architectures that **gcc** doesn't support natively. As an example, we will learn how to build a gcc cross-compiler for the **ARM-CORTEX** processor that the Raspberry Pi uses since it is widely gaining traction in the *Internet of Things*.

But, before we can cross-compile our operating system for the Raspberry Pi, we will begin by getting an existing cross-compiler that has been pre-built and ready for us to use. To do that, open a terminal prompt and run the following commands. These commands will create a directory to download our cross-compiler into, change directory into the newly created directory, download the cross-compiler, extract it, and rename the extracted folder for easier reference.

```
# sudo mkdir /opt
# cd /opt
# wget https://launchpad.net/gcc-arm-embedded/5.0/5-2015-q4-
major/+download/gcc-arm-none-eabi-5_2-2015q4-20151219-linux.tar.bz2
# sudo tar xjf gcc-arm-none-eabi-5_2-2015q4-20151219-linux.tar.bz2
# sudo mv gcc-arm-none-eabi-f_5_2-2015q4 arm-none-eabi
```

As you can see in the above commands, the download tarball includes a version number in the filename. To ensure you have the latest build, point your web browser to https://launchpad.net/gcc-arm-embedded/+download and check for the latest version number and latest download link. Just make sure you select the download for "Linux installation tarball".

Now that you have downloaded and extracted the ARM cross-compiler, all you have left to do is add it to your PATH environment variable so that you can easily reference it. To add the cross-compiler to your PATH variable, run the following command from a terminal prompt in CentOS. This command will ensure that the path to your ARM cross-compiler is always available, even after rebooting CentOS.

```
# echo export PATH=${PATH}:/opt/arm-none-eabi/bin
```

From now on, whenever you want to compile your operating system for the Raspberry Pi, all you have to do is prefix your gcc, as, ld, and objcopy utilities with "arm-none-eabi" in your Makefile like so.

```
ARCH=arm-none-eabi
CC=${ARCH}-gcc
AS=${ARCH}-as
LD=${ARCH}-ld
OBJCPY=${ARCH}-objcopy
```

Even though we now have a way to cross-compile our operating system to run on a Raspberry Pi, do not get too excited just yet. As we learned in earlier chapters, the code we developed for our bootloader, linker, and parts of our kernel are specific to the x86 architecture. In order to have our operating system run on the Raspberry Pi (or other architectures for that matter), we will need to modify our bootloader, kernel, and linker file to match the architecture we wish to run on.

Toward the end of this chapter, I have provided some sample code to help get you started with porting your operating system to run on the Raspberry Pi. But, before we get into that, I want to first show you how to build your own cross-compilers so that you will be armed with enough knowledge to build operating systems that can run on any architecture. And, since we are already on the path of cross-compiling for the Raspberry Pi, we will stick with this approach and learn how to build a custom cross-compiler from scratch that will be similar to the pre-built cross-compiler we previously downloaded. To do that, we will need to download and install yet another tool.

Create a Custom Cross-Compiler

The tool we will be using to create our own cross-compilers is called "crosstool-ng" (http://crosstool-ng.org). Begin by opening a terminal in CentOS and downloading the tool using the following commands.

```
# cd /tmp
# wget http://crosstool-ng.org/download/crosstool-ng/crosstool-ng-
1.22.0.tar.bz2
```

Note: At the time of writing this book, the release version of crosstool-ng is 1.22.0. It is recommended that you check the http://crosstool-ng.org website for the latest version and substitute the latest version number into the wget URL above. You will also need to use the same version in the commands below when unpacking the tool.

Next, you will need to run the following command to install a few dependencies that are required by the crosstool-ng installer.

```
# sudo yum -y install gcc-c++ glibc-devel glibc-static libstdc++* glibc.i686
# sudo yum -y install gperf bison flex texinfo libtool automake help2man
patch ncurses*
```

Next, run the following commands to unpack and install the crosstool-ng tool ("**ct**" hence forth).

```
# tar xjf crosstool-ng-1.22.0.tar.bz2
# cd crosstool-ng
# ./configure --prefix=/opt/cross
# make
# sudo make install
# sudo cp ct-ng.comp /etc/bash_completion.d/
# export PATH="${PATH}:/opt/cross/bin"
```

You can replace the path in the configure prefix above with a location that better suits you and your system, but make sure you also replace the path in the **PATH** environment variable as well.

Now that you have **ct** installed, it is time to use it. To begin with, we will need to create a new directory that will store the configuration files for **ct**. Once we have created that directory, we will change directory into it so that **ct** knows where to store its configuration files. From there, we can launch the tool.

sudo mkdir /opt/cross/toolchains
sudo mkdir /opt/cross/config
cd /opt/cross/config
sudo /opt/cross/bin/ct-ng menuconfig

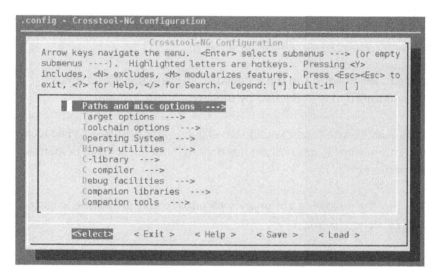

Using your arrow keys, you will need to traverse the configuration tool to make the following changes. Note: To select (enable/disable) items, press the spacebar. To edit text fields (such as the "Prefix directory", highlight the item and press enter.

- Paths and misc options

- Enable "Try features marked as EXPERIMENTAL"
  - Enable "Allow building as root user"
    - Enable "Are you sure?"
  - Change the "${HOME}/x-tools/${CT_TARGET}" Prefix directory to "/opt/cross/toolchains/${CT_TARGET}"
- Target options
  - Change the "Target Architecture" to "arm"
  - Leave "Endianness" as "Little endian"
  - Leave "Bitness" as "32-bit"
  - Set "Architecture level" as "armv6zk"
  - Set "Emit assembly for CPU" as "arm1176jzf-s"
  - Set "Tune for CPU" as "arm1176jzf-s"
  - Set "Use specific FPU" as "vfp"
  - Change "Floating point" to "hardware (FPU)"
  - Leave "Default instruction set mode" as "arm"
  - Make sure "Use EABI" is selected
- Toolchain options
  - Change "Tuple's vendor string" to "rpi"
- Operating system
  - Change "Target OS" to "linux"
- Binary utilities
  - Leave "Binary format" as "ELF"
  - Change "bintutils version" to "2.22"
- C compiler
  - Enable "Show Linaro versions"
  - Change the "gcc version" to "linaro-4.9-2015.06" (or whatever the latest linaro version is)
  - Set "gcc extra config" as "--with-float=hard"
  - Enable "C++"

After you have made your changes, be sure to save your changes before exiting the utility. The next thing we will do is tell **ct** to build our new cross-compiler. A word of warning, this can take quite a while to run. So, I would advise that you do this late at night, just before going to bed, or at another time when you have other things you can be doing while it runs.

If we try to build our cross-compiler without setting the flag "Allow building as root user" in the "Paths and misc options" menu above, it will complain about not having permissions to remove certain files. Even if we attempt to run the build process as sudo, it will complain with the error "You must NOT be root to run crosstool-NG". To get around this, we will need to either enable "Allow building as root user" in the config tool or change ownership of the folder and files for the configuration we did in the previous step. To do the latter, execute the following command and replace "USER:USER" with the name and group of the user you are currently logged in as.

sudo chown -R USER:USER /opt/cross/config
sudo chown -R USER:USER /opt/cross/toolchains

Next, begin the cross-compiler build while you find something else to do.

cd /opt/cross/config/
sudo /opt/cross/bin/ct-ng build

As mentioned before, this process will take a while to run. As you can see in the screenshot below, it took almost an hour (57 minutes, 58 seconds) to run on my laptop. I am also running a SSD (Solid State Drive) and 32GB of RAM with a 2.7GHz quad-core i7 processor. So, if you are running anything less, it will most likely take longer to complete on your system.

```
[INFO ]  ================================================================
[INFO ]  Extracting and patching toolchain components
[INFO ]  Extracting and patching toolchain components: done in 204.90s (at 05:45)
[INFO ]  ================================================================
[INFO ]  Installing GMP for host
[INFO ]  Installing GMP for host: done in 116.88s (at 07:42)
[INFO ]  ================================================================
[INFO ]  Installing MPFR for host
[INFO ]  Installing MPFR for host: done in 51.52s (at 08:34)
[INFO ]  ================================================================
[INFO ]  Installing ISL for host
[INFO ]  Installing ISL for host: done in 44.94s (at 09:19)
[INFO ]  ================================================================
[INFO ]  Installing CLooG for host
[INFO ]  Installing CLooG for host: done in 7.89s (at 09:26)
[INFO ]  ================================================================
[INFO ]  Installing MPC for host
[INFO ]  Installing MPC for host: done in 20.63s (at 09:47)
[INFO ]  ================================================================
[INFO ]  Installing binutils for host
[INFO ]  Installing binutils for host: done in 114.58s (at 11:42)
[INFO ]  ================================================================
[INFO ]  Installing pass-1 core C gcc compiler
[INFO ]  Installing pass-1 core C gcc compiler: done in 545.34s (at 20:47)
[INFO ]  ================================================================
[INFO ]  Installing kernel headers
[INFO ]  Installing kernel headers: done in 51.39s (at 21:38)
[INFO ]  ================================================================
[INFO ]  Installing C library headers & start files
[INFO ]  Installing C library headers & start files: done in 15.97s (at 21:54)
[INFO ]  ================================================================
[INFO ]  Installing pass-2 core C gcc compiler
[INFO ]  Installing pass-2 core C gcc compiler: done in 727.44s (at 34:02)
[INFO ]  ================================================================
[INFO ]  Installing C library
[INFO ]  Installing C library: done in 555.73s (at 43:18)
[INFO ]  ================================================================
[INFO ]  Installing final gcc compiler
[INFO ]  Installing final gcc compiler: done in 879.77s (at 57:57)
[INFO ]  ================================================================
[INFO ]  Cleaning-up the toolchain's directory
[INFO ]     Stripping all toolchain executables
[INFO ]  Cleaning-up the toolchain's directory: done in 2.20s (at 58:00)
[INFO ]  Build completed at 20160111.141923
[INFO ]  (elapsed: 57:58.65)
[INFO ]  Finishing installation (may take a few seconds)...
```

After the build process has completed, you will now have a compiler that will allow you to compile your operating system for the Raspberry Pi. However, there are a few changes we will need to make to our code before we can use the compiler.

To make it easy to get to our compiler, we will need to add its path to our **PATH** environment variable. So that this path is still available after we reboot, we will go ahead and make it permanent by using the following command.

echo export PATH=${PATH}:/opt/cross/toolchains/arm-rpi-linux-gnueabi/bin/ >> ~/.bashrc

Now, every time we want to call our cross-compiler, we can do so by typing just the compiler name itself which we can test with the following command.

arm-rpi-linux-gnueabi-gcc --version

output

arm-rpi-linux-gnueabi-gcc (crosstool-NG crosstool-ng-1.22.0) 4.9.4 20150629 (prerelease)
Copyright (C) 2015 Free Software Foundation, Inc.
This is free software; see the source for copying conditions. There is NO warranty; not even for MERCHANTABILITY or FITNESS FOR A PARTICULAR PURPOSE.

To see what compilers were built by crosstool-ng, you can simply list all the files in the toolchain directory using the following command.

ls /opt/cross/toolchains/arm-rpi-linux-gnueabi/bin/

Porting for the Raspberry Pi

Even though we now have new compilers for compiling our operating system for different architectures, there is still work to be done. As we learned before, Assembly code is written per architecture – meaning, code that is written for one architecture will not run on another. The same is also true for parts of our kernel (mostly the pieces that communicate directly with the hardware such as our graphics card) and the linker file we use to pull it all together. Therefore, in order for us to run our operating system on the Raspberry Pi like we now want to do, we will have to make several changes to our code.

However, since explaining how operating systems work for the Raspberry Pi requires an entire book itself, I will not be explaining it all here nor will I be providing the code here either. Instead, you can download the code directly from my website at http://www.lucuslabs.com/downloads/pi_os.zip.

Testing on Physical Hardware

Now that we have our operating system compiled to run on the Raspberry Pi, it is time to actually run it on the physical hardware. But, before we can do that, there are a couple of things we need to do to prepare.

First, we need to format our SD card with the correct partition type that our Raspberry Pi can understand. To do that, insert your SD card into your Windows computer and open Windows Explorer. Then, right-click on the drive for your SD card and select "Format...". In the dialog window that appears, select "FAT (Default)" for the "File system" and leave everything else as the defaults. When you are ready, click the "Start" button to format the card.

Next, open a web browser and navigate to http://www.lucuslabs.com/downloads/rpi_loader.zip. In this ZIP, you will find two files called "bootcode.bin" and "start.elf". These are the bootloader files required by the Raspberry Pi in order to boot your operating system.

You will need to extract these files from the ZIP and copy them into the root directory of the SD card you just formatted. Once you have done that, take the "kernel.img" file you built in the previous section over to your SD card. When done, your SD card's file structure should look like the following.

SD Card
bootcode.bin
kernel.img
start.elf

If your files look like the above, then your SD card is now ready to test. To do that, simply remove the SD card from your Windows computer and insert it into your Raspberry Pi. Next, connect the Raspberry Pi to a TV or monitor via the HDMI cable and power up the Pi by connecting a power source to the micro-USB port. At this point, you should now see your very own operating system displaying "Hello world" on your display.

Congratulations! You are now ready to take on the *Internet of Things*!

Conclusion

Throughout this book, we have covered a lot of ground. We started our journey by learning the basics about how operating systems work. Then we were introduced to machine code and the Assembly and C programming languages. The next steps of our journey showed us how to setup a virtualized development environment which we would next use to build our operating system, after which we did just that.

We started building our own operating system by writing a bootloader entry point using the Assembly programming language followed by building our very own kernel using C. Heck, we even followed a road that helped us start our architecture library and even expand our operating system just a bit. Plus, just for good measures, we even learned how to create our own cross-compilers and how to port our operating system to run on other devices such as the Raspberry Pi.

It has taken us quite a while to get here, but we have finally made it. We have now built our very own operating system and from here on, the possibilities are endless. So, I encourage you to now take what you have learned from this book and set out into the world to build some amazing technologies. As you do, I would like to ask that you share your story with me so that I too can follow your journey as you have followed mine. I look forward to using future technologies that you develop by first building your own operating system. The technology world is going to be a better place and you will be its leader. Congratulations and thank you!

Acknowledgements

First and foremost, I would like to thank my wife, Rita. This is the fifth book I have written in the last six months and she has stood by me during all five books. I can't count how many times I have stayed up late to work on my books, only to wake her when coming to bed. She is a great woman - especially for putting up with me. ☺

Second, I would like to thank Paul Brown, Chief Enterprise Architect at TIBCO Software Inc., for his feedback throughout the writing and editing process of this book. Paul has written several books of his own about Service Oriented Architecture (SOA) as well as architecting applications using TIBCO products, all of which are well worth the read.

Third, I would like to thank one of this book's readers, Stuart Gentry, who has graciously provided feedback about his first-hand experience while working through the book. Along with the corrections of several typos and other mistakes, additional notes have been added for further clarity based on the feedback Stuart has provided. Stuart has tremendous passion for cyber security, technology in general, and for helping HR locate candidates for our field. He is also man of Faith as well as a proud husband and father.

Lastly, I would like to thank my dog, Cheerio. Just like Rita, Cheerio has (literally) been by my side while writing my books this year. As Rita slept in bed and I worked late into the nights, Cheerio slept under my desk and never moved until I moved first. Crazy dog!

Appendix

Compiling the "Print Lucus" Example

In the "Intro to the Assembly Programming Language" chapter, I introduced you to a tiny application that prints my name, "Lucus", to the screen. Now that we have an environment for developing such code, it is time to show you how to write, compile, and execute that application.

To begin with, start up CentOS and click on **Applications > Accessories > gedit** which will launch a text editor where you can enter the below code. Once you have the code in gedit, you can save the file as whatever you want. For the demonstration purposes here, I have chosen to save my file as "**print_lucus.asm**" which we will reference shortly.

print_lucus.asm

```
section .text
global _start

_start:
    mov edx,len
    mov ecx,msg
    mov ebx,1
    mov eax,4
    int 0x80

    mov eax,1
    int 0x80

section .data
    msg db 'Lucus', 0xa
    len equ $ - msg
```

Before you can run the code above, you will first need to compile it. To do that, you can use the **nasm** utility mentioned in Chapter 5. The following command line will use that tool to compile the Assembly code above so that it can run on a 64-bit operating system (which is what our CentOS development environment is). If you want to compile the code to run on a 32-bit operating system, replace "**elf64**" with "**elf32**" or simply "**elf**" (which is shorthand for **elf32**).

nasm -f **elf64** print_lucus.asm

It is also possible to compile the code to run on other processors by replacing "**elf64**" with the format that matches your OS. To get a list of available formats, you can run the following command:

nasm -hf

For reference purposes, here is that list.

---

valid output formats for -f are ('*' denotes default):
* bin   flat-form binary files (e.g. DOS .COM, .SYS)
  ith   Intel hex
  srec   Motorola S-records
  aout   Linux a.out object files
  aoutb   NetBSD/FreeBSD a.out object files
  coff   COFF (i386) object files (e.g. DJGPP for DOS)
  elf32   ELF32 (i386) object files (e.g. Linux)
  elf64   ELF64 (x86_64) object files (e.g. Linux)
  elfx32   ELFX32 (x86_64) object files (e.g. Linux)
  as86   Linux as86 (bin86 version 0.3) object files
  obj   MS-DOS 16-bit/32-bit OMF object files
  win32   Microsoft Win32 (i386) object files
  win64   Microsoft Win64 (x86-64) object files
  rdf   Relocatable Dynamic Object File Format v2.0
  ieee   IEEE-695 (LADsoft variant) object file format
  macho32   NeXTstep/OpenStep/Rhapsody/Darwin/MacOS X (i386) object files
  macho64   NeXTstep/OpenStep/Rhapsody/Darwin/MacOS X (x86_64) object files
  dbg   Trace of all info passed to output stage
  elf   ELF (short name for ELF32)
  macho   MACHO (short name for MACHO32)
  win   WIN (short name for WIN32)

Once you have your code compiled, the next step will be to link the compiled output to an actual program that we can execute. To do that, you will need to run the following command, replacing "**print_lucus**" with the name of your application.

ld -s -o **print_lucus print_lucus**.o

To execute the program, all you have to do is prepend a **./** before the file name like so:

./print_lucus

After you compile the application as shown above, you can get the hexadecimal numbers from the example in the "Intro to Machine Code" chapter by executing the following command:

hexdump print_lucus

output

```
0000000 457f 464c 0102 0001 0000 0000 0000 0000
0000010 0002 003e 0001 0000 00b0 0040 0000 0000
0000020 0040 0000 0000 0000 00f0 0000 0000 0000
0000030 0000 0000 0040 0038 0002 0040 0004 0003
0000040 0001 0000 0005 0000 0000 0000 0000 0000
0000050 0000 0040 0000 0000 0000 0040 0000 0000
0000060 00cd 0000 0000 0000 00cd 0000 0000 0000
0000070 0000 0020 0000 0000 0001 0000 0006 0000
0000080 00d0 0000 0000 0000 00d0 0060 0000 0000
0000090 00d0 0060 0000 0000 0006 0000 0000 0000
00000a0 0006 0000 0000 0000 0000 0020 0000 0000
00000b0 06ba 0000 b900 00d0 0060 01bb 0000 b800
00000c0 0004 0000 80cd 01b8 0000 cd00 0080 0000
00000d0 754c 7563 0a73 2e00 6873 7473 7472 6261
00000e0 2e00 6574 7478 2e00 6164 6174 0000 0000
00000f0 0000 0000 0000 0000 0000 0000 0000 0000
*
0000130 000b 0000 0001 0000 0006 0000 0000 0000
0000140 00b0 0040 0000 0000 00b0 0000 0000 0000
0000150 001d 0000 0000 0000 0000 0000 0000 0000
0000160 0010 0000 0000 0000 0000 0000 0000 0000
0000170 0011 0000 0001 0000 0003 0000 0000 0000
0000180 00d0 0060 0000 0000 00d0 0000 0000 0000
0000190 0006 0000 0000 0000 0000 0000 0000 0000
00001a0 0004 0000 0000 0000 0000 0000 0000 0000
00001b0 0001 0000 0003 0000 0000 0000 0000 0000
```

```
00001c0 0000 0000 0000 0000 00d6 0000 0000 0000
00001d0 0017 0000 0000 0000 0000 0000 0000 0000
00001e0 0001 0000 0000 0000 0000 0000 0000 0000
00001f0
```

At this point, you should see a series of numbers laid out in equal rows and columns as shown in the output above. Now, I am sure you are probably thinking to yourself right now that what you are now looking at doesn't exactly match the numbers shown in the earlier chapter exactly, and there is a good reason for that. As mentioned earlier in this book, we learned that all software has to be loaded into memory before it can be executed. We also learned that memory is divided into multiple partitions and equal parts. Here, the code is broken into eight equal parts containing two bytes per part, equaling sixteen bytes per line. This is done because the **hexdump** utility defaults to using base-16 output.

The numbers in the column on the left are the numbers that are missing from the numbers shown earlier. These are the offsets that indicate how and where the application will be broken up when it gets loaded into memory and read by the CPU (i.e. the physical memory addresses). If you convert each of these hexadecimal values into decimals, you will notice that the first row begins at 0 and every row thereafter increments by 16 as shown below.

Another thing you will also notice is that there is an asterisk in the middle that separates two sections, the first being 16 rows and the second being 13 rows. This is done because, instead of repeating lines that contain the same data as the previous line, the **hexdump** utility replaces repeating lines (such as all zeros at the "240" / "00000f0" memory address) with an asterisk.

Below is the same code as above, but converted and displayed as decimal values in place of hexadecimal values.

output
```
0 17791 17996 258 1 0 0 0 0
16 2 62 1 0 176 64 0 0
32 64 0 0 0 240 0 0 0
48 0 0 64 56 2 64 4 3
64 1 0 5 0 0 0 0 0
80 0 64 0 0 0 64 0 0
```

```
 96 205 0 0 0 205 0 0 0
112 0 32 0 0 1 0 6 0
128 208 0 0 0 208 96 0 0
144 208 96 0 0 6 0 0 0
160 6 0 0 0 0 32 0 0
176 1722 0 47360 208 96 443 0 47104
192 4 0 32973 440 0 52480 128 0
208 30028 30051 2675 11776 26739 29811 29810 25185
224 11776 25972 29816 11776 24932 24948 0 0
240 0 0 0 0 0 0 0 0
*
304 11 0 1 0 6 0 0 0
320 176 64 0 0 176 0 0 0
336 29 0 0 0 0 0 0 0
352 16 0 0 0 0 0 0 0
368 17 0 1 0 3 0 0 0
384 208 96 0 0 208 0 0 0
400 6 0 0 0 0 0 0 0
416 4 0 0 0 0 0 0 0
432 1 0 3 0 0 0 0 0
448 0 0 0 0 214 0 0 0
464 23 0 0 0 0 0 0 0
480 1 0 0 0 0 0 0 0
496
```

Complete x86 Operating System Source

As a refresher, following are the files for the for the x86 operating system in
their entirety.

start.asm

```
bits 32
global _start
extern kernel_early
extern main

section .text
    align 4
    dd 0x1BADB002          ; magic
    dd 0x00                ; flags
    dd - (0x1BADB002 + 0x00) ; checksum

_start:
```

```
        cli
        mov esp, stack
        call kernel_early
        call main
        hlt

section .bss
resb 8192
stack:
```

kernel.c

```
static char* const VGA_MEMORY = (char*)0xb8000;

static const int VGA_WIDTH = 80;
static const int VGA_HEIGHT = 25;

void kernel_early(void) {
        // do some early work here
}

int main() {
        const char *str = "Hello world";
        unsigned int i = 0; // place holder for text string position
        unsigned int j = 0; // place holder for video buffer position

        while (str[i] != '\0') {
                VGA_MEMORY[j] = str[i];
                VGA_MEMORY[j + 1] = 0x07;
                i++;
                j = j + 2;
        }
        return 0;
}
```

linker.ld

```
ENTRY (_start)
SECTIONS
```

```
{
  . = 0x100000;
  .text : { *(.text) }
  .bss  : { *(.bss)  }
}
```

```
set timeout=0
set default=0
menuentry "My Cool OS" {
        multiboot /boot/myos
}
```

```
CC=gcc
TARGET=myos
C_FILES=./kernel.c
OBJS=$(C_FILES:.c=.o)

all compile: $(TARGET)
all: finale
.PHONY: all compile clean finale

%.o:
        $(CC) -c $(@:.o=.c) -o $@ -ffreestanding -fno-exceptions -m32

$(TARGET): $(OBJS)
        $(shell nasm -f elf start.asm -o start.o)
        $(CC) -m32 -nostdlib -nodefaultlibs -lgcc start.o  $? -T linker.ld -o
$(TARGET)

finale:
        $(shell cd ~/Desktop/my_os/)
        $(shell cp $(TARGET) ./iso/boot/$(TARGET))
        $(shell grub2-mkrescue iso --output=$(TARGET).iso)

clean:
        rm -f *.o $(TARGET)
```

```
find . -name \*.o | xargs --no-run-if-empty rm
```

Index

Made in the USA
Las Vegas, NV
04 June 2021

24194957R00085